AUSSIE JOKES

A 'True Blue' collection of
cheeky Australian jokes

Compiled by Tara Wyllie

CONTENTS

AUSSIE JOKES

Published by Brolga Publishing Pty Ltd
ABN 46 063 962 443
PO Box 12544
A'Beckett St
Melbourne,VIC, 8006
Australia

email: markzocchi@brolgapublishing.com.au

Copyright © 2016 Tara Wyllie
National Library of Australia Cataloguing-in-Publication
        Wyllie, Tara, author
        Aussie Jokes
        9781925367195 (paperback)
        Australian wit and humor.
        A827.108

Printed in Australia
Cover design & Typesetting by Brolga Publishing

BE PUBLISHED

Publish through a successful publisher. National distribution, Macmillan
& International distribution to the United Kingdom, North America.
Sales Representation to South East Asia
Email: markzocchi@brolgapublishing.com.au

THE AUSSIE
TRAVELLER

ELOCUTION LESSONS

A New Zealander walked into a Sydney fish shop and asked for some "Fush 'n' Chups."

"You're a Kiwi," said the proprietor.

The New Zealander was sick of being picked on for his accent, so he took some elocution lessons.

Six months later he went back to the same shop.

Feeling extremely confident, he walked in and asked, in perfect Oxford English, "Fish and Chips, please."

"You're a Kiwi," pronounced the proprietor.

"How the hell could you tell that?" asked the surprised New Zealander.

"Because this has been a hardware shop for four months."

BUSINESS TRIP

A Perth businessman went to Sydney for a week to buy stock for his store. His wife was very disappointed when told she could not accompany him.

At the end of the week, he telephoned her to say he would have to stay another week as he was still buying.

At the end of the second week, he again telephoned to say he would have to remain in Sydney as he was still buying.

"If you stay there another week, darling," said his wife, "I'll start selling what you're buying."

TWO PARACHUTES

A charter flight was carrying four passengers to Darwin. One was a businessman, one was a Bishop, one a backpacker and the other was the Prime Minister himself. Somewhere over the desert the pilot made an announcement that the plane was nearly out of fuel. He said there were only four parachutes and, apologising for being a coward, threw three of the parachutes into the cabin and jumped with the fourth.

The Bishop said he was an important man with a large diocese to look after, then grabbed a parachute and jumped.

The Prime Minister said he the most intelligent leader in history and must have a parachute, so he grabbed one and leapt from the plane.

The businessman said to the backpacker, "That leaves one parachute between the two of us."

"No it doesn't," said the backpacker. "We have a parachute each. The most intelligent leader in history has just jumped with my backpack."

SAVED BY A SAILOR

A young Melbourne woman was so depressed that she decided to end her life by throwing herself into the sea, but just before she threw herself from the wharf, a handsome young man stopped her.

"You have so much to live for," said the man. "I'm a sailor, and we're off to France tomorrow. I can stow you away on my ship. I'll take care of you, bring you food every day, and keep you happy."

With nothing to lose, combined with the fact that she had always wanted to go to France, the woman accepted.

That night the sailor brought her aboard and hid her in a small but comfortable compartment in the hold. From then on, every night he would bring her sandwiches, a bottle of red wine, and make love to her until dawn. Two weeks later she was discovered by the captain during a routine inspection.

"What are you doing here?" asked the captain.

"I have an arrangement with one of the sailors," she replied. "He brings me food and I get a free trip to France."

"I see," the captain said.

The woman's conscience got the best of her and she added, "Plus, he's screwing me."

"He certainly is," replied the captain. "This is the Tasmanian Ferry."

AUSSIE IN LONDON

A young Aussie bloke moved to London and went to Harrods looking for a job. The manager asked "Do you have any sales experience, young man?"

The young man answered, "Yeah, I was a salesman back home in Melbourne."

The manager liked the Aussie so he gave him the job. His first day on the job was challenging and busy, but he got through it.

After the store was locked up, the manager came down and asked, "How many sales did you make today?"

The Aussie said, "One!"

The manager groaned and continued, "Just one? Our sales people average 20 or 30 sales a day. How much was the sale for?"

"£124,237.64."

The manager choked and exclaimed "£124,237.64! What on earth did you sell?"

"Well, first I sold the customer a small fish hook, then a medium fish hook and then I sold him a new fishing rod. Then I asked him where he was going fishing and he said down at the coast, so I told him he would need a boat, so we went down to the boat department and I sold him that twin-engine Power Cat. Then he said he didn't think his Honda Civic would pull it, so I took him down to car sales and I sold him the 4WD Range Rover."

The manager, incredulous, said "You mean to tell me, a guy came in here to buy a fish hook and you sold him a boat and a 4WD?"

"No no no... he came in here to buy a box of tampons for his wife and I said... 'Well, since your weekend's ruined, you might as well go fishing.'"

LIVE-TO-AIR

The plane from Sydney was coming in to land.

"As soon as I clock off," the pilot said, not realising that he had forgotten to turn off the PA system, "I'm going to have a nice cold beer and get busy that hot flight attendant."

The horrified flight attendant made a dash toward the cockpit, but tripped over a suitcase in the aisle. A little old lady sitting in an aisle seat whispered, "There's no need to hurry, dear – he said he was going to have a beer first."

LARRYGATOR

Larry, a wealthy man in Florida, was famous for his parties. One evening, his guests were enjoying themselves as usual – dancing, eating superb seafood, drinking champagne. Then Larry announced that before the party he had a four metre long alligator placed in his pool. "I'll give half a million dollars to anyone who has the nerve to jump in," he dared. Just then there was an almighty splash and Fred the Aussie was fighting the alligator. Fred was punching and jabbing the alligator's eyes, head butting, kicking and biting him. Then he straddled the alligator and encircled his neck squeezing with all his might. The man and animal flipped round and round amid gushes of water, showering the goggle-eyed party goers. Groans and shrieks escaped from Fred and the alligator frantically thrashed the pool. Then suddenly it stopped and the corpse floated on top, while Fred painfully dragged himself out of the pool.

Larry rushed up to him. "Fred you're marvellous. You've earned your half a million."

"Don't bother," said Fred. "I don't want it."

"What? Fred, what do you mean? I've got to reward you. How about a house then?"

"No. Really, I don't want it."

"How about a Rolls?"

"No. There's only one thing I want."

"Tell me. Anything."

"Who was the son of a b**** who pushed me in?!"

NINE MONTHS LATER

Dave and Aaron were travelling out bush when their car broke down. They approached a farmhouse and the widow, Dot, fed them and put them up for the night. About nine months later Dave rang Aaron.

"Remember the night the car broke down out in the country?" he asked.

"Yeah?" said Aaron.

"You didn't by any chance slip into the widow's bedroom, did you?"

Aaron admitted that he had. "You didn't by any chance use my name, did you Azza?" asked Dave. Aaron admitted that he had and said he was sorry.

"Don't worry about it, Az," said Dave. "I've just got a letter from a legal firm that says she died and left me the farm. Want to come with me to the funeral?"

FIRING SQUAD

An Aussie, an Englishman and an Irishman were arrested in America for smuggling.

"You will be shot at dawn tomorrow," the captain of the police force said. The three had a restless night.

"Don't worry, chaps," said the Englishman. "I shall invoke the natural disaster plan. These Americans are terrified of natural disasters. Just watch me." At dawn the Englishman said he would face the firing squad first and the other two watched from their cells as the captain said, "Ready... Aim..."

"Earthquake! Earthquake!" roared the Englishman at the top of his voice. The Americans panicked and in the confusion the Pommie escaped. Later the Aussie was led to the wall and the captain said, "Ready... Aim..."

"Flood! Flood!" roared the Aussie, and in the confusion he escaped too. The Irishman had picked up the drift of the plot. It was all a matter of timing, so he listened as the captain ordered, "Ready... Aim..."

"Fire! Fire!" yelled the Irishman.

COUNTING SHEEP

A starving hitchhiker was going past a farm one day, saw the farmer.

He said, "I bet you I can tell you how many sheep are in your paddock."

"I bet you can't," said the farmer.

"If I can guess correctly, will you give me a sheep?"

"Sure!" said the farmer.

"There are 5,918 sheep," said the hitchhiker.

"How did you do that?" said the amazed farmer.

"I can't tell you, but can I have my animal please?"

The hitchhiker picked up an animal and began to walk off.

"Just a moment," called the farmer. "If I can tell you what profession you used to have, can I have my animal back?"

"Sure," said the hitchhiker.

"You're an accountant."

"Christ... how did you know that?"

"I can't tell you," said the farmer. "But can I have my dog back?"

HIT THE ROAD JACK

A Northern Territory jackaroo is overseeing his herd when suddenly a brand-new red BMW emerges out of a dust cloud and screams to a stop.

The driver, a young man in a designer suit and sunglasses, leans out the window and says to the jackaroo, "If I tell you how many sheep you have, will you give me a lamb?"

The jackaroo looks at the man, obviously a yuppie, then looks at his peacefully grazing herd and calmly answers, "Sure, why not?"

The yuppie parks his car, whips out his notebook computer, connects it to his mobile phone, and surfs the Internet, where he calls up a GPS satellite to get the exact fix on his location which he then feeds to another satellite that scans the area in an ultra-high-resolution photo.

The young man then opens the digital photo and exports it to an image processing facility. In seconds, he receives an email that the image has been processed and the data stored. He then accesses database through a spreadsheet with email on his smart phone and, after a few minutes, receives a response.

Finally, he prints out a full-colour, 150-page report on his hi-tech, miniaturised LaserJet printer, turns to the farmer and says, "You have exactly 1,586 sheep and lambs."

"That's right. Well, I guess you can take one of my lambs," says the jackaroo.

He watches the young man select one of the animals and looks on bemused as the young man stuffs it into the trunk of his car.

Then the jackaroo says to the young man, "Hey, if I can tell you exactly what your business is, will you give me back my lamb?"

The young man thinks about it for a second and then says, "Okay, why not?"

"You work for the Australian Government," says the jackeroo.

"Wow! That's correct," says the yuppie, "but how did you guess that?"

"No guessing required," answered the jackeroo. "You showed up here even though nobody called you; you want to get paid for an answer I already knew, to a question I never asked. You used all kinds of expensive equipment that clearly somebody else has paid for. You tried to show me how much smarter than me you are; and you don't know a thing about sheep. This is a herd of cattle. Now give me back my dog."

TAXI!

David was telling his wife about his first business trip to London. He had some spare time so took a taxi to get a feel of the city.

After an hour he decided he'd like to stop at a hotel for a drink. He tapped the taxi driver on the shoulder to get his attention.

The driver screeched, lost control of the taxi, nearly hit a car, swerved up a footpath, just missed a pedestrian and stopped inches from a large shop window.

For a few moments there was deathly silence. Then, the driver gasped, "Are you alright? I'm terribly sorry, but you scared the sh★★ out of me."

David whispered, "I'm so sorry for startling you. I had no idea that a tap on the shoulder would scare you like that."

The driver replied, "No. It was my fault. I'm terribly sorry. Today's my first day driving a taxi. I've been driving a hearse for 10 years."

FLIGHT FUEL

Aircraft mechanics Cazza and Bazza were mates who'd worked together for years at Hobart Airport.

One day a particularly heavy fog closed the airport and the mates had nothing to do. They were so bored that Cazza said, "Hey Baz, I wish we could have a drink."

"Me too," said Bazza. "Hey we could try some jet fuel. I hear it gives you a real high."

"Great. Let's give it a go."

The mates poured some jet fuel in their mugs and found it a good drop. Before long they were as drunk as skunks.

The next day Cazza woke up with no hangover. Fantastic!

Then his 'phone rang. "Caz. How'ya goin'?" asked Bazza.

"Great!" said Cazza. "I don't have a hangover. How're you goin'?"

"Good as gold," said Bazza.

"Good one! Let's do it again," said Cazza.

"Er, there's just one thing," said Bazza.

"What?"

"Have you farted yet?"

"No."

"Well I have. And I'm in Darwin!"

BREAKING IT DOWN IN PLAIN ENGLISH

Here's the final word on nutrition and health following an exhaustive review of the research literature.

- Japanese eat very little fat and suffer fewer heart attacks than us.

- Mexicans eat a lot of fat and suffer fewer heart attacks than us.

- Chinese drink very little red wine and suffer fewer heart attacks than us.

- Italians drink excessive amounts of red wine and suffer fewer heart attacks than us.

- Germans drink beer and eat lots of sausages and fats and suffer fewer heart attacks than us.

– The French eat *foie-gras*, full fat cheese and drink red wine and suffer fewer heart attacks than us.

CONCLUSION: Eat and drink what you like and stop speaking English, because that's what seems to kill you.

LOST IN TRANSLATION

At lunch time two Italian secondary school students in Melbourne, Orico and Piedro, talk animatedly at a table near a female student who is reading while eating. After a few moments she loses concentration when she hears Orico saying, "Effa come first, then I come, then Ella come, then I come, then pee, then I come, then Enna then Oh come, then Arse come lasta.

The girl is shocked. She says, "I'm going to report you for your foul language and talking about your sex lives in the school canteen."w

Orica says, "Hey, whate are you talking aboute? 'I'm justa helping Piedro spella Filipinos, for his geography exams."

JOKES FOR
THE BLOKES

MY SHOUT

Pete and Richard, from country Victoria, bought a Tatts ticket together and won. They decided to go to Melbourne to collect it in cash.

After collecting their winnings they were walking down Flinders Street when Pete turned to Richard and said, "I'm hungry, Dick, do you fancy a pie?"

"Sure," said Richard. So Pete bought two pies.

A bit further, they came to a car showroom. Richard said, "Why don't we get ourselves a new car each?"

"Okay," said Pete.

The salesman pointed to two sparkling new cars.

"These BMWs are worth $125,000 each," he said.

"We'll take two," said Richard.

Pete started to get some cash out but suddenly stopped. He punched Richard on the shoulder and said, "Oh I almost forgot, it's your shout. I got the pies."

TAKE WHAT YOU WANT

Jason was telling his flatmate about his exciting day.

"This gorgeous woman in a BMW convertible picked me up and drove me to her apartment, then she took off all her clothes and said I could have anything I wanted."

"How exciting! What did you do?" asked the flatmate.

"I took the car, but none of her clothes fitted me," said Jason

DOES YOUR DOG BITE?

Kym was standing at the bar with a rottweiler at his feet.

"Does your dog bite, Kym?" asked Mick.

"No," replied Kym. So Mick went to pat the dog. The dog just about tore off Mick's arm. "I thought you said your dog didn't bite!"

"That's not my dog," replied Kym.

KNICKERS

Late one night Bill said to his mate Ben, "When I get home, I'm gonna rip my wife's undies off."

"Why's that?" asked Ben.

"The elastic is killing me," he replied.

DEEP SEA BUSINESS

Darren had taken scuba-diving lessons and it was his first time to dive without an instructor.

He was on the sea bed when he saw a man coming towards him in a grey flannel suit, collar and tie, carrying a briefcase.

He could hardly believe his eyes, so he got his underwater board and chalk and wrote, "What are you doing down here?"

The guy grabbed the chalk and scribbled, "I'm drowning you bloody idiot!"

BRAVERY

The young reporter had been assigned to do the annual story on General Miles.

"He has the reputation of being Australia's bravest soldier," said the editor. "The story has been done before, but if you can find a new angle, your career will take off."

The young reporter went off to the old soldiers' home with the comments of the editor still ringing in his ears.

"If only there was a time the general had been scared," he thought.

The young reporter found the general sitting in his wheelchair on the veranda and soon came to the point.

"Surely, sir, there was a time when you were frightened?"

The general looked thoughtful. "Well," he began, "there was a time I was in the jungle and this rogue tiger had eaten two or three of the native chaps. I remember I tracked the beast through the jungle and got a glimpse of him hiding behind some tall grass. I cocked my gun and crept right up to the grassy patch and I was about to peep through the grass when that tiger leapt straight at me and roared, 'Aaaarrrgh!' My God, I shit myself."

The cadet whipped out his notebook. "So you were so scared of the lion you crapped in your pants?" he asked, intrigued.

"No, it was just then when I went 'aaaarrrgh'," said the general.

PRETENCE

There was a loser who couldn't get a date. He went to a bar and asked this one guy how to get a date.

The guy said, "It's simple. I just say, I'm a lawyer."

So the guy went up to a pretty woman and asked her out. After she said "No," he told her that it was probably a good thing because he had a case early in the morning.

She said, "Oh! You're a lawyer?"

He said, "Why... Yes I am!"

So they went to his place and when they were in bed, having sex, he started to laugh to himself. When she asked what was so funny, he answered, "Well, I've only been a lawyer for fifteen minutes, and I'm already screwing someone!"

PAST IT

The old bloke with a walking stick made it shakily into the brothel. The receptionist looked him over and noting his age said, "Just a moment, I had better call the Madam."

After a whispered conference the Madam nodded agreement and said to the old guy, "Sorry love, but we think you've had it."

"Oh, sorry, how much do I owe you?" the old boy said, reaching for his wallet.

THE AUSSIE WAY

A Somalian man is given permission to live in Australia.

Jabril rents and moves into a small house near Mildura, Victoria. A few days later Kev, the friendly next door neighbour, decides to visit and welcome him. But walking up the drive he sees the Somalian running around his front yard in circles chasing several hens. Not wanting to interrupt these Somalian practises, Kev decides to welcome him the next day.

The next morning Kev tries again, but just before he knocks on the front door, he sees through the window the Somalian man urinating into a glass and then drinking it!

"Blimey what a strange custom," he thought. He wanted to be culturally sensitive so decided to welcome his neighbour another day.

The third day he tries again. But 'lo and behold!' he sees his new neighbour leading a bull down the driveway and then put his head next to the bull's bum.

Kev can't take any more and marches up to his neighbour and says, "Hey Mate, what is it with your customs? I come to welcome you to the neighbourhood, and see you running around in circles after hens. Then the next day you're pissing in a glass - and drinking it! Now you had your head so close to that bull's bum, it could shit on you."

The Somalian (who learnt English while he was in the Detention Centre) is amazed and says, "Sorry sir, you not understand, these are not Somalian ways. I doing Australian customs."

"What do you mean mate?" asks Kev. "Those aren't Aussie ways."

"Yes they are. Back home I learnt on TV," replied Jabril. "Man say to become true Australian, I learn chase chicks, drink piss, and listen to bullshit."

ARMED FORCES

A tough old Sergeant Major found himself at a university gala event. Many young idealistic women attended the event and one started speaking with him.

"Excuse me, Sergeant Major, but you seem to be a very serious man. Is something bothering you?" she asked.

"Negative, ma'am. Just serious by nature."

The young woman looked at his awards and decorations and said, "You've seen a lot of action."

"Yes, ma'am, a lot of action."

The young woman, tiring of trying to start up a conversation, said, "You know, you should lighten up. Relax and enjoy yourself."

The Sergeant Major just stared at her in his serious manner.

Finally the young lady said, "You know, I hope you don't take this the wrong way, but when is the last time you had sex?"

"1955, ma'am."

"Well, that's why you're so serious. You really need to chill out! I mean, no sex since 1955!"

She took his hand and led him to a private room where she proceeded to "relax" him several times.

Afterwards, panting for breath, she leaned against his bare chest and said, "Wow, you sure didn't forget much since 1955."

The Sergeant Major said, after glancing at his watch, "I hope not; it's only 2130 now."

SPARKY

A bright spark was sent on his way to Heaven. Upon arrival, a concerned St Peter met him at the Pearly Gates.

"I'm sorry," St Peter said, "But Heaven is suffering from an overload of goodly souls and we have been forced to put up an Entrance Exam for new arrivals to ease the burden of Heavenly Arrivals."

"That's cool," said the bright spark. "What does the Entrance Exam consist of?"

"Just three questions," said St Peter.

"Which are?" asked the bright spark.

"The first is:" said St Peter, "which two days of the week start with the letter 'T'? The second is: how many seconds are there in a year? The third is: what was the name of the swagman in Waltzing Matilda? Now," said St Peter, "I'll give you a couple of hours to think about these and then I'll ask you for the answers."

So the bright spark gave those three questions much thought.

When time was up St Peter asked, "Which two days of the week start with the letter T?"

The bright spark said, "Today and tomorrow."

St Peter pondered this answer and decided that indeed the answer could be applied to the question.

"Well then, what's your answer to the second question –how many seconds in a year?"

The bright spark replied, "Twelve!"

"Only twelve?" exclaimed St Peter, "How did you arrive at that number?"

"Easy," said the bright spark, "there's the second of January, the second of February, right through to the second of December, giving a total of twelve seconds."

St Peter looked at the bright spark and said, "I need some time to consider your answer before I can give you a decision."

But after a few minutes, St Peter returned to the bright spark and said. "I'll allow the answer to stand, but you need to get the final question absolutely correct to be allowed into Heaven."

"What was the name of the swagman in Waltzing Matilda?"

The bright spark replied, "That's the easiest question. It was Andy of course."

"Really?!"

This flabbergasted St Peter. "How did you arrive at THAT answer?"

"Easy," said the bright spark, "Andy sat, Andy watched, Andy waited 'til his billy boiled."

And lo, the bright spark entered Heaven...

TECH SUPPORT

Dear Tech Support,

Last year I upgraded from Boyfriend to Husband and noticed a slowdown in system performance, particularly in the flower and jewellery applications, which operated flawlessly under Boyfriend.

Also, Husband uninstalled many other valuable programmes, such as Romance and Personal Attention and then installed undesirable programs such as: Football, Cricket and Going to the Pub with Mates. Conversation no longer runs, and Housecleaning simply crashes the system. I've tried running Nagging to fix these problems, but with no success.

What can I do?

Signed, Desperate

Dear Desperate,

First keep in mind, Boyfriend is an Entertainment Package, while Husband is an Operating System. Please enter the command: 'http: I Thought You Loved Me.html' and try to download Tears.

Don't forget to install the Guilt update. If that application works as designed, Husband should then automatically run the applications Jewellery and Flowers, but remember - overuse of the above application can cause Husband to default to Grumpy Silence, Garden Shed or Beer. Beer is a very bad program that will download the Snoring Loudly.

Whatever you do, DO NOT install Mother-in-law (it runs a virus in the background that will eventually seize control of all your system resources). Also, do not attempt to reinstall the Boyfriend program. These are unsupported applications and will crash Husband.

In summary, Husband is a great system, but it does have limited memory and cannot learn new applications quickly. It also tends to work better running one task at a time. You might consider buying additional software to improve memory and performance. We recommend Food and Hot Lingerie.

Good Luck,

Tech Support

DEAR GOD

There was a man who worked for the Post Office processing the mail that had illegible addresses.

One day, a letter came addressed in a shaky handwriting to God with no actual address. He thought he should open it to see what it was about.

The letter read:

Dear God,

I am an 80 year old widow, living on a very small pension.

Yesterday someone stole my purse. It had $100 in it, which was all the money I had until my next pension payment.

Next Sunday is Christmas, and I had invited two of my friends over for dinner. Without that money, I have nothing to buy food with, have no family to turn to, and you are my only hope. Can you please help me?

Sincerely,

Edna

The postal worker was touched. He showed the letter to the other workers. Each one dug into his or her wallet and came up with a few dollars.

By the time he made the rounds, he had collected $96, which they put into an envelope and sent to the woman. The rest of the day, all the workers felt a warm glow thinking of Edna and the dinner she would be able to share with her friends.

Christmas came and went.

A few days later, another letter came from the same old lady to God.

The workers gathered around while the letter was opened. It read:

Dear God,

How can I ever thank you enough for what you did for me?

Because of your gift of love, I was able to fix a glorious dinner for my friends. We had a very nice day and I told my friends of your wonderful gift.

By the way, there was $4 missing.

I think it might have been those misers at the post office.

Sincerely,

Edna

IMPRESSED

A drover from a huge cattle station in outback Australia appeared before St. Peter at the Pearly Gates.

"Have you ever done anything of particular merit?" St. Peter asked.

"Well, I can think of one thing," the drover offered. "On a trip to the backblocks of Broken Hill in New South Wales, I found a bikie gang who were threatening a young sheila. I told them to leave her alone, but they wouldn't listen. So I approached the largest and most heavily tattooed bikie and smacked him in his face, kicked his bike over, ripped out his nose ring, and threw it on the ground. I yelled, 'Now, back off!! Or I'll kick the sh★★ out of the lot of ya!'"

St. Peter was impressed. "When did this happen?" "A couple of minutes ago."

DAY AT THE RACES

One Saturday on a bad day at the race track, Colin noticed a priest stepping onto the track and blessing the forehead of one of the horses lining up for the 4th race. Amazingly that horse – who was a very long shot - won the race.

Before the next race, as the horses began lining up, Colin again saw the priest approaching a horse and blessing it on the forehead. Colin thought he couldn't do any worse than he had been all day so he put a small bet on that horse, although it was not a favourite. Sure enough it won!

When Colin saw the priest bless another horse, he rushed off to back it and was rewarded with another win. Then followed several more races before which each time the priest blessed an unpopular horse and Colin, now feeling confident, made big bets followed by wins for each long shot.

This was more exciting than any of Colin's wildest dreams and he decided to seize the moment. He withdrew all his savings from the ATM and awaited the priest's blessing.

It was clear the next race was going to be another winner because this time Colin saw the priest blessing the eyes, ears, and hooves of an old nag. So Colin placed all his money on it.

But to his dismay, he saw the old nag lurch towards the starting line and drop dead.

Colin was shocked and raced to the priest. "Father!" Colin

shouted. "What's gone wrong? All day you've blessed horses who then won. But for this race, the horse you blessed has dropped dead. Because of you, I've lost all my money. I'm ruined."

The priest looked at Colin sympathetically. "My son, you must be a Protestant, because you can't tell the difference between a blessing and the Last Rites!"

HITCHING A RIDE

On a very dark night in the midst of a big storm, John Bradford, a Sydney University student, was on the side of the road hitchhiking. The storm was so strong he could hardly see in front of him...Suddenly, he saw a car slowly coming towards him and stop. John, desperate for shelter, jumped into the car and closed the door only to realize there was nobody behind the wheel and the engine wasn't on.

The car started moving slowly. John looked at the road ahead and saw a curve approaching. Scared, he started to pray, begging for his life. Then, just before the car hit the curve, a hand appeared out of nowhere through the window and turned the wheel. John, was paralyzed with terror, but the hand that had come through the window, had not touched or harmed him.

Shortly after John saw the lights of a pub appear down the road. Gathering strength, he jumped out of the car and ran towards the pub. Wet and out of breath, he rushed inside and started telling everybody about the horrible experience he had just had.

A silence enveloped the pub when everybody realized he was crying and... wasn't drunk.

Suddenly, the door opened, and two other people walked in from the wild, stormy night. They, like John, were also soaked and out of breath. Looking around, and seeing John Bradford sobbing at the bar, one said to the other, "Look Paddy, there's the idiot who got in the car while we were pushing it!"

EVENING CLASSES FOR MEN

DAY ONE
HOW TO FILL ICE CUBE TRAYS
Step by step guide with slide presentation
TOILET ROLLS: DO THEY GROW ON THE HOLDERS?
Roundtable discussion
DIFFERENCES BETWEEN LAUNDRY BASKET & FLOOR
Practicing with hamper (pictures and graphics)
DISHES: DO THEY LEVITATE/FLY TO KITCHEN SINK OR WASH BY THEMSELVES?
Debate among a panel of experts.
REMOTE CONTROL
Losing the remote control - Help line and support groups
LEARNING HOW TO FIND THINGS
Starting with looking in the right place instead of turning the house upside down while screaming - Open forum

DAY TWO
EMPTY MILK CARTONS: DO THEY BELONG IN THE
FRIDGE OR THE BIN?
Group discussion and role play
HEALTH WATCH: BRINGING HER FLOWERS IS NOT
HARMFUL TO YOUR HEALTH
PowerPoint presentation
REAL MEN ASK FOR DIRECTIONS WHEN LOST
Real life testimonial from the one man who did
IS IT GENETICALLY IMPOSSIBLE TO SIT QUIETLY AS
SHE PARALLEL PARKS?
Driving simulation
LIVING WITH ADULTS: BASIC DIFFERENCES
BETWEEN YOUR MOTHER AND YOUR PARTNER
Online class and role playing
HOW TO BE THE IDEAL SHOPPING COMPANION
Relaxation exercises, meditation and breathing techniques
REMEMBERING IMPORTANT DATES & CALLING
WHEN YOU'RE GOING TO BE LATE
Bring your calendar to class
GETTING OVER IT: LEARNING HOW TO LIVE WITH
BEING WRONG ALL THE TIME
Individual counsellors available

WITTY

AUSSIE WOMEN

MOTHER-OF-THE-BRIDE

Catherine's wedding day was fast approaching. Nothing could dampen her excitement – not even her parent's nasty divorce. She had spent days helping her mother, Diana, to find the most amazing dress to wear.

Diana would be the best dressed mother-of-the-bride ever!

A week later, Catherine was horrified to learn that her father's new young wife had bought the exact same dress!

Catherine asked her to exchange it, but she refused:

"Absolutely not, I look like a million bucks in this dress, and I'm wearing it."

Catherine informed her mother who graciously said, "Never mind sweetheart. I'll get another dress. After all, it's your special day."

A few days later, they went shopping again and found another gorgeous dress. Catherine asked her mother, "Aren't you going to return the other dress? You really don't have another occasion where you could wear it."

Diana just smiled and replied, "Of course I do, dear. I'm wearing it to the rehearsa dinner the night before the wedding."

WRONG OBJECT

A secretary was sitting at her desk with a tampon behind her ear. The boss came through and said, "Sharon, what on earth is that behind your ear?"

She felt it and said, "My God, what have I done with my pen?"

CHIHUAHUA

A young woman was advised that her miniature show dog would never win a prize because its hair was too long; it was supposed to be a smooth hair breed. So she went to the chemist for some hair remover. The chemist handed her a tube of the latest product. "When you put this on, it's best to keep your arms up for at least three minutes," he said.

"Oh, you misunderstand," she said, rather embarrassed. "It's not for my underarms, it is for my Chihuahua."

"Well in that case," said the chemist, "don't ride a bike for half an hour."

TOO MUCH SEX

A woman was complaining to her friend that she was tired all the time. "How often do you have sex?" asked the friend.

"Monday, Wednesday and Saturday," she replied.

"Well, cut out Saturday," said the friend.

"I can't," she said. "That's the night with my husband."

FREE MEAT

It was fifteen years since a pretty little girl had come into the shop of Don the Butcher with the news that the baby she was carrying was his. Don agreed to provide her with free meat until the child was fifteen.

When the boy came to collect the next lot of meat, Don said, "You'll be fifteen tomorrow. You can tell your mother that this is the last lot of meat she will be getting from me. Then watch the expression on her face!"

The boy repeated this to his mother and she replied, "Son, go back to the butcher and tell him I've had free groceries and free fruit and vegetables for the last fifteen years, and watch the expression on his face!"

INSIGNIFICANT DETAIL

Mary's wedding day was approaching and all the arrangements were made but she was worried that all would not go well.

"You know," she said to her mother, "the whole thing could be ruined if we overlook some insignificant detail."

"Don't worry," Mary's mother assured her. "I'll make sure he's there."

SHOE SIZE

Two young wives were having their morning coffee and the conversation was about men.

"It's not fair," said Julie, "men can look at us and tell how we're equipped physically, but we can't tell how well a man is equipped unless we go to bed with him."

"Of course we can," replied Sue. "Look at his feet."

"His feet?"

"Yes. The bigger his feet, the bigger his penis."

"I didn't know that," said Julie.

"What size shoe is your husband?" asked Sue.

"Size eight."

"Well, go to bed with a man who wears a different size and you can make the comparison."

A few days later a young electrician called at the house to carry out some work. Julie looked at him thoughtfully and asked, "What size shoes do you wear?"

"Size ten. Why do you ask?" laughed the young man.

"Well, my husband got a new pair of size eight shoes that he doesn't like and I thought they might fit you."

"Too bad. Wrong size."

The electrician ended up in bed with Julie. Later as he prepared to leave, she handed him $100.

"Don't be silly, I wanted to do it with you," he said.

"Oh, it's not for going to bed with me," explained Julie.

"It's to buy a new pair of shoes. The ones you are wearing are far too small, they must be killing you!"

POSITIONS PLEASE

Three heavily pregnant women were sitting in a cafe, drinking tea.

"I know what sex I'm going to have," Antonia announced proudly. The other two asked how she knew.

She replied, "Well I was on top when I conceived so I will have a boy."

Jacqui said, "If that is true then I will have a girl because I was on the bottom when I conceived."

Caroline started to cry, ordered a whiskey and wailed, "Puppies! I'm going to have puppies!"

WATCH WHAT YOU SAY

A woman was sitting at a bar, enjoying an after work cocktail with her girlfriends, when an exceptionally tall, handsome, sexy young man entered. The woman could not take her eyes off him.

The young man noticed her staring and walked towards her. Before she could offer her apologies for being rude and staring, the young man said to her, "I'll do anything, absolutely anything that you want me to do, no matter how kinky, for $100, on one condition."

Flabbergasted, she asked what the condition was.

The young man replied, "You have to tell me what you want me to do in just three words." The woman considered his proposition for a moment, withdrew from her purse five $20 notes, which she slowly counted into the young man's outstretched hand.

She looked deeply into his eyes and slowly, meaningfully, said, "Clean my house."

HOW WOMEN COMMUNICATE:

1. Fine: This is the word women use to end an argument when they are right and you need to shut up.
2. Five Minutes: If she is getting dressed, this means half an hour. Five minutes is only five minutes if you have just been given five more minutes to watch the footy before mowing the lawn.

3. Nothing: This is the calm before the storm. This means something, and you should be on your toes. Arguments that begin with nothing usually end in 'fine'.

4. Go Ahead: This is a dare, not permission. Don't Do It!

5. Loud Sigh: This is actually a word, but is a non-verbal statement often misunderstood by men. A loud sigh means she thinks you are an idiot and wonders why she is wasting her time standing here and arguing with you about nothing. (Refer back to 3 for the meaning of nothing.)

6. That's Okay: This is one of the most dangerous statements a women can make to a man. That's Okay means she wants to think long and hard before deciding how and when you will pay for your mistake.

7. Thanks: A woman is thanking you, do not question, or faint. Just say you're welcome. (I want to add in a clause here – this is true, unless she says Thanks a lot – that is PURE sarcasm and she is not thanking you at all. DO NOT say you're welcome. That will bring on a whatever).

8. Whatever: Is a woman's way of saying 'Go to Hell'.

9. Don't worry about it, I got it: Another dangerous statement, meaning this is something that a woman has told a man to do several times, but is now doing it herself. This will later result in a man asking What's wrong? For the woman's response, refer to 3.

FIRST CLASS BLONDE

A plane is on its way to Darwin, when a blonde in economy class stands up and moves to the first class section and sits. The flight attendant sees her do this and asks to see her ticket. She then tells the blonde that she paid for economy class so she will have to go back to her old seat.

The blonde replies, "I'm blonde, I'm beautiful, I'm going to Darwin and I'm staying right here."

The flight attendant goes into the cockpit and tells the pilots that there's a blonde bimbo sitting in first class who should be sitting in economy class and refuses to return to her seat. The co-pilot goes to the blonde and tries to explain that because she only paid for an economy class seat she will have to return to it.

The blonde replies, "I'm blonde, I'm beautiful, I'm going to Darwin and I'm staying right here."

The co-pilot tells the pilot that he probably should radio the police to arrest the blonde when they land. The pilot says, "You say she's blonde? I'll handle this. I'm married to one and I speak blonde."

He goes to the blonde and whispers in her ear. She says "Oh, I'm so sorry," and returns to her seat in economy class.

The flight attendant and co-pilot are astounded and ask him what he said to make her return to her seat.

"I told her that first class isn't going to Darwin."

CASINO DISTRACTION

A beautiful woman walked into a small casino just as it was about to close and said she wanted to gamble $2000 on one roll of the dice. Deciding that the odds were in their favour, the two owners agreed. The woman put down her money and they put down theirs.

"Just a moment," she said. She went to the ladies room and came out a little later, stark naked and rolled the dice.

"Seven," she said, picked up her money, returned to the ladies room, dressed and left. "Did you see that seven?" the fist man said to the other.

"No," he replied, "Did you?"

EXTRA LARGE

A young woman walked into a chemist and asked the young man behind the counter where the extra large condoms were. The clerk looked at her, shrugged and said, "They're right over here," showing her to them.

The woman thanked the sales assistant and stood there beside them, and stood there, and stood there.

The assistant asked her, "Is there something else I can help you with?"

The woman smiled sweetly at him and said, "No, thank you. I'm just waiting here to see who buys them."

AGES

Several girlfriends in their forties discussed where they should meet for dinner. Finally, it was agreed that they should meet at the Ocean View restaurant because the waiters there wore tight pants.

Ten years later in their fifties, the friends again discussed where they should meet for dinner. Finally they decided to meet at the Ocean View restaurant because the food and wine selections were very good.

Ten years later in their sixties, the women again discussed where they should meet for dinner. They finally agreed that they should meet at the Ocean View restaurant because they could eat there in peace and quiet and, above all, the restaurant had a beautiful ocean view.

Ten years later in their seventies, the group yet again discussed where they should meet for dinner. Finally it was agreed that they should meet at the Ocean View restaurant because the restaurant was wheel chair accessible and had an elevator.

Ten years later in their eighties, the friends again discussed where they should meet for dinner. Finally it was agreed that they should meet at the Ocean View restaurant because they had never been there before.

BATTLE OF THE SEXES

A woman arrived at the Gates of Heaven. While she waited for Saint Peter to greet her, she peeked through the gates. She saw a beautiful banquet table. Sitting all around were her parents and all the other people she had loved and who had died before her.

They saw her and began calling to her:

"Hello – How are you?"

"We've been waiting for you!"

"Good to see you."

When Saint Peter came by, the woman said to him, "This is

such a wonderful place! How do I get in?"

"You have to spell a word," Saint Peter told her.

"Which word?" the woman asked.

"Love."

The woman correctly spelled 'Love', and Saint Peter welcomed her into Heaven.

About a year later, Saint Peter came to the woman and asked her to watch the Gates of Heaven for him that day.

While the woman was guarding the Gates of Heaven, her husband arrived.

"I'm surprised to see you," the woman said. "How have you been?"

"Oh, I've been doing pretty well since you died," her husband told her.

"I married the beautiful young nurse who took care of you while you were ill.

"And then I won the multi-state lottery.

"I sold the little house you and I lived in and bought a huge mansion.

"And my wife and I travelled all around the world. We were on holiday in Hawaii and I went water skiing today. I fell and hit my head, and here I am. What a bummer! How do I get in?"

"You have to spell a word," the woman told him.

"Which word?" her husband asked.

"Czechoslovakia..."

A WISE BLONDE

A blonde and her husband are lying in bed listening to the next door neighbour's dog... It has been barking in the backyard for hours and hours. The blonde jumps out of bed and says,
"I've had enough of this," and goes downstairs.

The blonde finally comes back to bed and her husband says, "The dog is still barking, what have you been doing?"

The blonde smiles triumphantly and says,

"I put the dog in our backyard. Let's see how they like it!"

FAMILY CALLS

Leslie the blonde goes into work one morning crying her eyes out. Her boss asks sympathetically, "What's the matter?"
Leslie replies, "Early this morning I got a phone call saying that my mother had passed away."

The boss, feeling sorry for her, says, "Why don't you go home for the day? Take the day off to relax and rest."

"Thanks, but I'd be better off here. I need to keep my mind off it and I have the best chance of doing that here."

The boss agrees and allows her to work as usual.

A couple of hours pass and the boss decides to check on Leslie.

He looks out from his office and sees her crying hysterically.

"What's so bad now? Are you going to be okay?" he asks.

"No!" exclaims Leslie the blonde. "I just received a horrible call from my sister. Her mother died, too!"

DOUBLE TROUBLE

Two blondes Shaz and Maz are walking down the street.

One notices a compact on the sidewalk and leans down to pick it up.

She opens it, looks in the mirror and says, "Hmm, this person looks familiar."

The second blonde says, "Here, let me see!" So the first blonde hands her the compact.

The second one looks in the mirror and says, "You dummy, it's me!"

TOILET TALK

Travelling on the Princes Highway and needing to use the toilet, I stopped at a rest area and headed to the toilet.

I'd hardly sat down when I heard a voice from the next cubicle saying, "Hi, how are you?"

I'm not the type to start a conversation in the toilet and I don't know what got into me, But I answered, somewhat embarrassed, "I'm fine!"

And the other person says, "So what are you up to?"

What kind of question is that? At that point, I'm thinking this is too bizarre so I say, "Uhhh, I'm like you, just traveling!"

Now I'm trying to get out as fast as I can when I hear another question. "Can I come over?"

Ok, this question is just too weird for me but I thought I'd be polite and end the conversation, so I say,

"No ... I'm a little busy right now!!!"

Then I hear the person say nervously, "Listen, I'll have to call you back. There's an idiot in the other cubicle who keeps answering all my questions."

DISCRIMINATION

A young ventriloquist is performing at the Melbourne Comedy Festival and with his puppet he goes through his usual repertoire of dumb blonde jokes.

Suddenly, a blonde woman in the front row stands and shouts, "Stop those insulting, stupid blonde jokes. How dare you stereotype blonde women that way! Hair colour has nothing to do with a person's intelligence. It's men like you who strip women like me of respect. This attitude is like a cancer that prevents us from full equality at work and positions of honour. You're not only discriminating against blondes but against women in general."

The chastened ventriloquist hastens to apologise, but the blonde interrupts him and yells, "It's not you I'm talking to but that dwarf on your lap."

DEAR DIARY

Dear Diary,

For my birthday this year, my dear daughter bought me a week of personal training at the local health centre. I booked the training with a personal trainer named David. The club encouraged me to keep a Diary to chart my progress.

Monday:

Started my day at 6:00 a.m. Tough to get out of bed, but found it was well worth it when I arrived at the health club to find David waiting for me. He's like a Greek god - with blonde hair, dancing eyes and a dazzling white smile. Wow! David was encouraging as I did my sit-ups, although my gut ached from holding it in while he was around. This is going to be a great week!

Tuesday:

I drank a pot of coffee and finally made it out the door. David made me lie on my back and push a heavy iron bar into the air then he put weights on it! My legs were a little wobbly on the treadmill, but I made the full mile. David's rewarding smile made it all worthwhile. I feel great!

Wednesday:

The only way I can brush my teeth is by laying the toothbrush on the counter and moving my mouth back and forth over it. I believe I have a hernia in both pectorals. Driving was okay as long as I didn't try to steer or stop.

David was impatient with me, insisting that my screams bothered other club members. His voice is a little too perky for early in the morning and when he scolds he gets this nasally whine that is VERY annoying. My chest hurt when I got on the treadmill, so David put me on the stair monster. Why the hell would anyone invent a machine to simulate an activity rendered obsolete by elevators? David told me it would help me get in shape and enjoy life.

Thursday:

David was waiting for me with his vampire-like teeth exposed as his thin, cruel lips were pulled back in a full snarl. I couldn't help being half an hour late. It took me that long to tie my shoes. David took me to work out with dumbbells. When he wasn't looking, I ran and hid in the toilet. He sent some skinny bitch to find me. Then as punishment he put me on the rowing machine – which I sank.

Friday:

I hate that David more than any human being has ever hated any other human being in the history of the world. Stupid, anaemic, anorexic creep. If there was a part of my body I could move without unbearable pain, I would beat him with it. David wanted me to work on my triceps. I don't have any triceps! And if you don't want dents in the floor, don't hand me the damn barbells or anything that weighs more than a sandwich. The treadmill flung me off and I landed on a health and nutrition teacher. Why couldn't it have been someone softer, like the drama coach or the choir director?

Saturday:

David left a message on my answering machine in his grating, shrilly voice wondering why I did not show up today. Just hearing him made me want to smash the machine with my planner. However, I lacked the strength to even use the TV remote and ended up catching eleven straight hours of the Weather Channel.

Sunday:

I've asked the Church van to pick me up for services today so that I can thank God that this week is over. I will also pray that next year my daughter will choose a gift for me that is fun -- like a root canal or a hysterectomy. I still say if God had wanted me to bend over, he would have sprinkled the floor with diamonds.

IMPORTANT MESSAGE

A very attractive woman goes up to a bar in a quiet rural pub. She gestures alluringly to the bartender who comes over immediately. When he arrives, she seductively signals that he should bring his face closer to hers. When he does she begins to gently caress his full beard. "Are you the manager?" she murmurs, softly stroking his face with both hands.

"Er, no," the man replies.

"Can you get him for me? I need to speak to him," she says, running her hands beyond his beard and into his hair.

"I'm afraid I can't," breathes the bartender. "Is there anything I can do?"

"Yes, there is. I need you to give him a message," she continues, running her forefinger across the bartender's lips and slyly popping a couple of her fingers into his mouth and allowing him to suck them gently.

"What should I tell him?" the bartender manages to say.

"Tell him," she whispers, "there is no toilet paper, hand soap, or paper towel in the ladies room."

HUBBY & THE MISSUS

BREAKFAST BANTER

A woman was making a breakfast of fried eggs for her husband. Suddenly, her husband burst into the kitchen.

"Careful," he said, "Careful! Put in some more butter! Oh my gosh! You're cooking too many at once. Too many! Turn them! Turn them now! We need more butter. Oh my gosh! Where are we going to get more butter? They're going to stick! Careful. Careful! I said be careful! You never listen to me when you're cooking! Never! Hurry up! Are you crazy? Have you lost your mind? Don't forget to salt them. You know you always forget to salt them. Use the salt! Use the salt! The salt!"

The wife stared at him. "What in the world is wrong with you? You think I don't know how to fry a couple of eggs?"

The husband calmly replied, "I just wanted to show you what it feels like when I'm driving."

MIRACLE

Johnson came back into bed and told his wife he'd just seen a miracle. "When I went to the bathroom the light came on all by itself, then when I'd finished the light went off all by itself," he said.

"No miracle," replied his wife. "You're drunk and you just pissed in the refrigerator!"

DEVIOUS

Doug was out with his mistress one night and he fell asleep. He was reluctant to call home as he knew his wife would guess what he'd been up to. Then he had an idea.

He rang his wife; "Don't pay the ransom," he shouted down the phone. "I escaped."

THE MISSUS

Three Aussie blokes Curley, Coot and Bluey are working on a mobile phone tower when they knock off for a smoko.

As they descend, Coot slips, falls off the tower and dies instantly.

As the ambulance takes the body away, Bluey says, "Blimey, someone's gotta tell Coot's missus."

Curley says, "OK, I'm pretty good at that sensitive stuff. I'll do it."

Two hours later, he comes back carrying a slab of beer. Bluey says, "Where'd you get the grog, Curley?"

"Coot's wife gave it to me," Curley replies.

"Well blow me down. You told the missus her hubby was dead and she gave you a slab of beer?"

"Well, not exactly," Curley says. "When she answered the door, I said to her, "You must be Coot's widow."

She said, "You must be mistaken... I'm not a widow."

Then I said, "I'll betcha a slab of beer you are..."

YOU CAN COUNT ON IAN

Jackie was sick of her old rattletrap car and often complained about it to her husband, Ian.

Not long before her birthday, she said, "Buy me a surprise for my birthday! Something that accelerates from 0 to 100 in 4 seconds! And I'd like a red one!" Happy and excited, Jackie counted down the days to her birthday. Finally, she got the beautiful present Ian had thoughtfully bought her. Red bathroom scales!

Apparently Ian is dead now....

BANK ROBBER

A man walked into a bank, stood in line, and when he reached the counter he pulled out a gun and robbed the bank.

Just to make sure there were no witnesses, he turned around and asked the next customer in line, "Did you see me rob this bank?"

The customer replied "Yes, I did!"

The bank robber raised his gun, pointed it to his head and shot him dead.

He moved to the next customer in line and said loudly to this man, "DID YOU SEE ME ROB THIS BANK?"

The man calmly responded, "No, I didn't, but my wife did!"

BOX UNDER THE BED

Richard and Julie were married for 40 years.

When they first got married Richard said, "I am putting a box under the bed. You must promise never to look in it." In all their 40 years of marriage Julie never looked. However, on the afternoon of their 40th anniversary, curiosity got the best of her. Inside the box were three empty beer cans and $2473.85 in cash. She closed the box and put it back under the bed.

Now that she knew what was in the box, Julie was doubly curious. That evening they were out for a special dinner. After dinner Julie could no longer contain her curiosity and she confessed, saying, "I am so sorry. For all these years I kept my promise and never looked into the box under our bed. However, today the temptation was too much and I gave in. But now I need to know why do you keep the cans in the box?"

Richard thought for a while and said, "I guess after all these years you deserve to know the truth. Whenever I was unfaithful to you I put an empty beer can in the box under the bed to remind myself not to do it again." Julie was shocked, but said, "I am very disappointed and saddened but I guess after all those years away from home on the road, temptation does happen and I guess that three times is not that bad considering the years." They hugged and made their peace.

A little while later Julie asked Richard, "Why do you have all that money in the box?"

Richard answered, "Whenever the box filled with empties, I cashed them in."

HOLIDAY ALONE

Joe and his wife always went on holiday together, so he was surprised and annoyed when, after complaining she was feeling run down, she advised him that she was going to Fiji for two weeks with her friend Gwen.

Towards the end of the holiday she e-mailed her Joe and said, "Am feeling a new woman. Do you mind if I stay another week?"

Joe replied, "So am I. Stay two!"

PHONE A FRIEND

Several men are changing in the golf club locker room. A mobile phone on a bench rings and Bob engages the hands-free speaker function and begins to talk. Everyone else in the room stops to listen.

Bob: "Hello."

Woman: "Hi darl, it's me. Are you at the club?"

Bob: "Yes."

Woman: "I'm at the shops and found this beautiful leather coat. It's only $1,000. Is it okay if I buy it?"

Bob: "Sure, go ahead if you like it that much."

Woman: "I also stopped by the Mercedes dealership and saw the latest models. There was one I really liked."

Bob: "How much?"

Woman: "$90,000."

Bob: "Okay, but for that price you'd want it with all the options."

Woman: "Great! Oh, and one more thing... I was just talking to Glenda and found out that the house I wanted last year is back on the market. They're asking $980,000 for it."

Bob: "Well, make an offer of $900,000. They'll probably take it."

Woman: " Okay. I'll see you later! I love you so much!"

Bob: "Bye!" Bob hangs up. The other men in the locker room stare at him in astonishment, jaws dropping. He turns and asks, "Anyone know whose phone this is?"

IN LOVING MEMORY

Bert died. His will provided $40,000 for an elaborate funeral. As the last guests departed, his widow Pat turned to her oldest and dearest friend.

"Ah well, Bert would be pleased," she said.

"You're right," replied Frances, who lowered her voice and leaned in close.

"So go on, how much did this really cost?"

"All of it," said Pat. "$40,000."

"No!" Frances exclaimed, "It was very grand, but $40,000?"

Pat answered, "The funeral was $6,500. I donated $500 to the church. The whisky, wine and finger food were another $500. The rest went for the Memorial Stone."

Frances computed quickly. "For the love of God Pat, $32,500 for a Memorial Stone? How big is it?"

"Take a look," said Pat as she held out her hand to display her new enormous diamond ring.

SIZE MATTERS

A man was sitting on the edge of the bed, observing his wife, looking at herself in the mirror.

Since her birthday was not far off he asked what she'd like to have for her birthday.

"I'd like to be twelve again," she replied, still looking in the mirror.

On the morning of her birthday, he arose early, made her a nice big bowl of Coco Pops, and then took her to Luna Park.

What a day!

He put her on every ride in the park: the Death Slide, the Corkscrew, the Wall of Fear, the Screaming Monster Roller Coaster, everything there was.

Six hours later they staggered out of the theme park. Her head was reeling and her stomach felt upside down.

He then took her to a McDonalds where he ordered her a Happy Meal with extra fries and a chocolate shake.

Then it was off to the pictures with popcorn, a huge Coca Cola, and her favourite sweets... M&Ms. What a fabulous adventure!

Finally she wobbled home with her husband and collapsed into bed exhausted.

He leaned over his wife with a big smile and lovingly asked, "Well dear, what was it like being twelve again?"

Her eyes slowly opened and her expression suddenly changed. "I meant my dress size, you twit!!!"

HAPPY COUPLE

A couple is lying in bed. The man says, "I'm going to make you the happiest woman in the world."

The woman replies, "I'll miss you."

CROTCHLESS KNICKERS

Trudie bought a pair of crotchless knickers in an attempt to spice up her dead sex-life. She put them on, together with a short skirt and sat on the sofa opposite her husband. Now and then she would cross and uncross her legs. Eventually her husband asked, "Are you wearing crotchless knickers?"

"Yes I am," she answered, seductively.

"Thank goodness for that. I thought the stuffing was coming out of the sofa!"

BLOODY SHIRT

A man walked into a dimly lit bar and the bartender asked him "Why is the front of your shirt all bloody?"

The customer answered in a slurred voice, "My wife caught me with another woman and cut off my penis."

"Oh come on," replied the bartender.

The customer then told him, "If you don't believe me, I'll show you." He began to rifle through his suitcase and pulled out something long and thin and he laid it on the bar.

The bartender bent down and looked at it closely and said, "Why this is just a cigar."

The customer looked puzzled and said, "I have it here somewhere," and proceeded to fumble through his other pockets and pulled out something else that was long and thin and placed it on the bar.

"See that?" he announced.

The bartender again inspected it closely and snapped, "You stupid dickhead, that's just another cigar."

The customer staggered backward and steadied himself, leaning on the bar and with a sudden awareness in his shaky voice said, "Son of a b★★★★, I must have smoked it!"

ACCORDING TO RESEARCH

A new sign in the Bank reads:

Please note that this Bank is installing new Drive-through ATM machines enabling customers to withdraw cash without leaving their vehicles.

Customers using this new facility are requested to use the procedures outlined below when accessing their accounts.

After months of careful research, MALE & FEMALE Procedures have been developed. Please follow the Appropriate steps for your gender.'

MALE PROCEDURE:
1. Drive up to the ATM.
2. Lower your car window.

3. Insert card into machine and enter PIN.
4. Enter amount of cash required.
5. Retrieve card, cash and receipt.
6. Raise window.
7. Drive off.

FEMALE PROCEDURE:
1. Drive up to ATM machine.
2. Reverse and back up the required amount to align car window with the machine.
3. Put hand brake on, put the window down.
4. Find handbag, remove all contents on to passenger seat to locate card.
5. Tell person on mobile phone you will call them back and hang up.
6. Attempt to insert card into machine.
7. Open car door to allow easier access to machine due to its excessive distance from the car.
7. Insert card.
8. Re-insert card the right way.
9. Dig through handbag to find diary with your PIN written on the inside back page.
10. Enter PIN
11. Press cancel and re-enter correct PIN.
12. Enter amount of cash required.
13. Check makeup in rear view mirror.
14. Retrieve cash and receipt.
15. Empty handbag again to locate purse and place cash inside.
16. Drive forward three feet.

17. Reverse back to ATM machine.
18. Retrieve card.
19. Re-empty hand bag, locate card holder, and place card into the slot provided.
20. Give dirty look to irate male driver waiting behind you.
21. Restart stalled engine and drive off.
22. Redial person on mobile phone.
23. Drive for three to four kilometres.
24. Release hand brake.

FERRIS WHEEL

A married couple went to the Melbourne Show. Cindy said he wanted to go on the Ferris Wheel but Bruce was too scared, so Cindy went on her own. The wheel went round and round. Suddenly Cindy's seat was thrown off the wheel and he landed in a heap at Bruce's feet.

"Are you hurt, Cindy?" Bruce asked anxiously.

"Of course I'm hurt! Three times round and you didn't wave once."

GLORY DAYS

When Gloria arrived at the breakfast table in an old chenille dressing gown and her hair in rollers, her husband asked her, "Why can't you look like you did when I married you?"

"Because I'm not pregnant now," she replied.

BIRTH CONTROL APPLIANCE

Brendan's wife, mother of twelve kids, called in to tell the doctor that she wouldn't be coming back as an expectant mother any more now that she had her birth control appliance.

The doctor was puzzled because what she indicated as her 'appliance' was an ordinary hearing aid.

"Before I had it," she explained, "we would get into bed at night and Brendan would say: 'Will we put out the light and go to sleep, or what?' And I would say, "What?'"

THE WRONG EMAIL ADDRESS

A man was away on a business trip in Queensland and wanted to send an email to his wife who was joining him the following day. Unable to and the scrap of paper on which he had written her email address, he did his best to type it in from memory. Unfortunately, he missed one letter, and his note was directed instead to an elderly vicar's wife whose husband had passed away only the day before. When the grieving widow checked her email, she took one look at the monitor, let out a piercing scream, and fell to the poor dead. At the sound, her family rushed into the room and saw this note on the screen:

Dearest Wife,
Just got checked in. Everything prepared for your arrival tomorrow.
Your Loving Husband.
P.S. Sure is hot down here.

HUBBY FOR SALE

A store that sells new husbands has opened in Sydney. Among the instructions at the entrance is a description of how the store operates:

You may visit this store ONCE ONLY!

Husband Store: There are six floors and the value of the products increases as the shopper ascends the flights.

The shopper may choose any item from a particular floor, or may choose to go up to the next floor, but you cannot go back down except to exit the building!

So, a woman goes to the Husband Store to find a husband.

On the first floor the sign on the door reads:

Floor 1 - These men Have Jobs.

She's intrigued, but continues to the second floor.

Floor 2 - These men Have Jobs and Love Kids.

"That's nice," she thinks, "but I want more." So she continues upward.

Floor 3 - These men Have Jobs, Love Kids, and are Extremely Good Looking.

"Wow," she thinks, but feels compelled to keep going.

Floor 4 - These men Have Jobs, Love Kids, are Drop-dead Good Looking and Help With Housework.

"Oh, mercy me!" she exclaims, "I can hardly stand it!" Still, she goes to the fifth floor.

Floor 5 - These men Have Jobs, Love Kids, are Drop-dead Gorgeous, Help with Housework, and Have a Strong Romantic Streak.

She is so tempted to stay, but she goes to the sixth floor.

Floor 6 - You are visitor 31,456,012 to this floor. There are no men on this floor. This floor exists solely as proof that women are impossible to please.

Thank you for shopping at the Husband Store.

PLEASE NOTE:

To avoid gender bias charges, the store's owner opened a New Wives store just across the street.

The first floor has wives that love sex.

The second floor has wives that love sex, have money and like beer.

The third, fourth, fifth and sixth floors have never been visited.

BARGAIN

A husband and wife are shopping at their local supermarket. The husband picks up a case of beer and puts it in their cart.

"What do you think you're doing?" asks the wife. "They're on sale, only $10 for 12 cans," he replies.

"Put them back, we can't afford them," demands the wife, and so they carry on shopping.

A few aisles further along the woman picks up a $20 jar of face cream and puts it in the basket.

"What do you think you're doing?" asks the husband.

"It's my face cream. It makes me look beautiful," replies the wife.

Her husband answers, "So do 12 cans of beer and they're half the price."

COUCH POTATO

Overworked, harassed wife sees her couch potato husband and asks him,

"What are you doing?"

"Nothing," he replies.

"But you did that yesterday."

"I haven't finished," he says.

PROMISES

On his death bed a man said to his wife, "Promise me that when I die you will put all my money in the coffin with me, because I want to have it with me in the afterlife." She did so, and soon after he died.

During the funeral service his wife sat beside her best friend in whom she had confided her promise to her husband.

After the ceremony and just before the undertakers closed the coffin, the wife said, "Wait!" She then placed a box in the coffin. The undertakers locked the casket and they rolled it away.

The friend said, "Myrtle, surely you weren't foolish enough to put all your money in there with your husband."

Myrtle replied, "I'm a faithful Catholic, so I cannot go back on my word. I promised him that I was going to do so and I did. I got it all together, put it into my account, and wrote him a cheque.... If he can cash it, then he can spend it."

REQUESTS

A man is watching the footy on TV when his wife interrupts.

"Darling, would you please fix the dripping tap in the kitchen? It's not working."

He replies impatiently, "Fix the dripping tap? Am I a plumber?"

The wife asks, "Well then would you mow the grass? It looks like a jungle."

To which he says, "Mow the grass? Am I a gardener? Hardly. I don't think so."

"Ok," she says.

"Well would you please wash the car? It's so filthy we can't see out the window."

"I'm not a cleaner and I don't want to wash the car. I'm sick of your nagging. I'm going to the pub."

So he goes to the local pub and watches the footy there with his mates. But when the game's over he feels guilty about his rudeness to his wife.

So he decides to apologise and returns home.

As he opens the front gate, he notices the lawn looking trim. Then notices the car is glistening! When he gets a beer he notices that the kitchen tap is silent.

"Sweety," he asks. "How come the grass is cut, the car is clean and the tap isn't dripping?"

She explains, "After you left I sat on the front verandah and cried. Then a sweet young man asked me what the matter was. I told him and he offered to do all the jobs. In return all he asked for was for me to go to bed with him or to bake him a cake."

The husband said, "So what kind of cake did you bake him?"
She replied, "Bake a cake? Am I a baker?"

THERAPY

Eileen and her husband Bob went for counselling after 30 years of marriage.

When asked what the problem was, Eileen went into a passionate, painful tirade listing every problem they had ever had in the 30 years they had been married.

She went on and on and on: neglect, lack of intimacy, emptiness, loneliness, feeling unloved and unlovable, an entire laundry list of unmet needs she had endured over the course of their marriage.

Finally, after allowing this to go on for a sufficient length of time, the therapist got up, walked around the desk and after asking Eileen to stand, embraced her, unbuttoned her blouse and bra, put his hands on her breasts and massaged them thoroughly, while kissing her passionately as her husband Bob watched with a raised eyebrow!

Eileen shut up, buttoned up her blouse, and quietly sat down while basking in the glow of being highly aroused.

The therapist turned to Bob and said, "This is what your wife needs at least three times a week. Can you do this?"

Bob thought for a moment and replied, "Well, I can drop her off here on Mondays and Wednesdays but on Tuesdays, Thursdays and Fridays I play bowls..."

PUSHING IT

A couple are awakened at 2 a.m. by a loud knocking on the front door. Mike gets out of bed and goes to the door where a drunken stranger, standing in the pouring rain, asks for a push.

"No, it's 2 a.m.," says Mike. He slams the door and returns to bed.

"Who was that?" asks his wife, Jan.

"Oh a drunk asking for a push," he answers.

"Did you help him?" she asks.

"No, I did not. It's 2 a.m. in the morning and it's pouring rain out there!"

"Well, you have a short memory," says Jan. "Can't you remember last year when we broke down, and that man helped us? I think you should help him, and you should be ashamed of yourself! God loves drunk people too you know."

Mike does as he is told, gets dressed, and goes out into the pounding rain.

He calls out into the dark, "Hello, are you still there?"

"Yes," comes the answer.

"Do you still need a push?" calls out Mike.

"Yes, please!" comes the reply from the dark.

"Where are you?" Mike asks.

"Over here on the swing," replies the drunk.

CAR TROUBLE

A couple, Phil and Carol, drove to the shopping centre, where their car broke down in the car park. Phil told Carol to do the shopping while he fixed the car. Carol returned later to see several people standing round the car. As she came closer she saw a pair of hairy legs sticking out from under the car.

Unfortunately the lack of underpants revealed normally private parts hanging out the side of his shorts.

Carol quickly stepped forward, put her hand up his shorts, and tucked everything back into place.

On regaining her feet, she looked across the bonnet and found herself staring at her husband, who was standing by watching. The mechanic however, had to have six stitches in his forehead.

PANTS MAN

Barry was going to marry Sandra, so his father sat him down for a man to man talk. "Barry let me give you the secret to the success of my marriage with your mother. On my wedding night I took off my pants, handed them to your mother, and said, 'Here - try these on.' She did and said, 'These are too big, I can't wear them.' I replied, 'Exactly, I wear the pants in this family and I always will.' Ever since that night we never had any problems."

"Hmmm," said Barry. He thought that might be worth trying. On his honeymoon, Barry took off his pants and said to Sandra, "Here - try these on."

She tried them on and said, "These are too large. They don't fit me." Barry said, "Exactly. I wear the pants in this family and I always will. I don't want you to ever forget that."

Then Sandra took off her pants and handed them to Barry. She said, "Here - you try on mine."

He did and said, "I can't get into your pants."

Sandra said, "Exactly. And if you don't change your attitude, you never will."

THE CAMERONS

A woman was in bed with her lover when she heard her husband opening the front door.

"Hurry," she said, "stand in the corner. She rubbed baby oil all over him, then dusted him with talcum powder.

"Don't move until I tell you," she said. "Pretend you're a statue."

"What's this?" the husband inquired as he entered the room.

"Oh, it's a statue," she replied, "the Camerons bought one and I liked it so I got one for us, too."

No more was said, not even when they went to bed. Around 4 am the husband got up, went to the kitchen and returned with a sandwich and a beer.

"Here," he said to the statue, "have this. I stood like that for two days at the Cameron's and nobody offered me a damned thing."

50 YEARS

St Peter's Catholic Church in Adelaide has weekly 'Husbands' marriage seminars. At the session last week, the priest asked an elderly Italian man named Giuseppe, who said he was approaching his 50th wedding anniversary, to take a few minutes and share some insight into how he had managed to stay married to the same woman all those years.

Giuseppe replied to the assembled husbands, "Wella, I'va tried to treat her nice, spenda da money on her, but besta of all is, I tooka her to Italy for the 25th anniversary!"

The priest responded, "Giuseppe, you are an inspiration to all the husbands here! Please tell us what you are planning for your wife for your 50th anniversary?"

Giuseppe proudly replied, "I gonna go pick her upa."

THE FOUR LETTER WORD

A young couple married and went on their honeymoon. Soon after their return, the new wife Sarah rang her mother.

"Well," said her mother, "how was the honeymoon?"

"Oh Mama," Sarah replied, "it was wonderful! *So* romantic, and he's... he's..." Suddenly she burst into tears. "As soon as we returned, Sam started using the most horrible language. Things I'd never heard before..." sobbed Sarah.

"I mean, all these *awful* four-letter words! You've got to take me home! *Please* Mama!" Sarah wailed.

"Sarah, *Sarah!*" her mother said. "Calm down! You need to stay with your husband and work this out. Now, tell me, what could be so awful? WHAT four-letter words?"

"*Please* don't make me tell you, Mama," wept the daughter.

"I'm *so* embarrassed; they're just too awful! JUST COME GET ME... *PLEASE!*"

"Darling, baby, you must tell me what has upset you so. Tell your mother those horrible four-letter words!"

Sobbing, Sarah said, "Oh, Mama!!! He used words like: "DUST... WASH... IRON... and COOK!!!""

DATES

Wife: "What are you doing?"

Husband: "Nothing."

Wife: "Nothing...? You've been reading our marriage certificate for an hour."

Husband: "I was looking for the expiry date."

DEVOTION

A woman's husband had been slipping in and out of a coma for several months. Yet she had stayed by his bedside every single day.

One day, when he came to, he motioned her to come nearer. As she sat by him, he whispered, eyes full of tears, "You know what? You've been with me through all the bad times. When I was fired, you were there to support me. When my business failed, you were there. When I was shot, you were by my side. When we lost the house, you stayed right here. When my health started failing, you were still by my side... You know what May?"

"What dear?" she gently asked, smiling as her heart began to fill with warmth.

"I'm beginning to think you're bad luck..."

ON THE CARDS

Marriage is like a deck of cards. In the beginning all you need is two hearts and a diamond.
By the end, you wish you had a club and spade.

SLEEP ON IT

"Darling how many women have you slept with?" a woman asks her husband one day.

"Only you, darling." her husband proudly replies, "With all the others I was awake."

WAKE UP CALL

A man and his wife were having some problems at home and were giving each other the silent treatment. Suddenly, the man realised that the next day, he would need his wife to wake him at 5:00 am for an early morning business flight. Not wanting to be the first to break the silence (and LOSE), he wrote on a piece of paper: *Please wake me at 5:00 am.*

He left it where he knew she would find it. The next

morning, the man woke up, only to discover it was 9:00 am and he had missed his flight. Furious, he was about to go and see why his wife hadn't wakened him, when he noticed a piece of paper by the bed. The paper said:

It's 5:00am. Wake up.

EGGCELLENT

She was standing in the kitchen, preparing our usual soft-boiled eggs and toast for breakfast, wearing only the 'T' shirt that she normally slept in. As I walked in, almost awake, she turned to me and said softly,

"You've got to make love to me this very moment!" My body shook and I thought, "I'm either still dreaming or this is going to be my lucky day!"

Not wanting to lose the moment, I embraced her and then gave it my all; right there on the kitchen table. Afterwards she said,

"Thanks," and returned to the stove, her T-shirt still around her neck.

Happy, but a little puzzled, I asked, "What was all that about?" She explained, "The egg timer's broken."

NOT A BAT IDEA

A married woman decided that she needed to pep up her sex life. So she arranged for the kids to stay overnight at Grandma's.

She took a long scented-oil bath and then put on her best perfume. She slipped into a tight leather bodice, a black garter belt, black stockings and six-inch stilettos. She finished it off with a black mask, ready for action.

When her husband got home from work, he grabbed a beer and the remote, sat down and yelled, "Hey, Batman, what's for dinner?"

SEPARATE BEDROOMS

Robert, 85, marries Jenny, a lovely 25 year old. Since her new husband is so old, Jenny decides that after their wedding she and Robert should have separate bedrooms, because she is concerned that her aged husband might over-exert himself if they spent the entire night together.

After the wedding festivities Jenny prepares herself for bed and the expected knock on the door.

Sure enough the knock comes, the door opens and there is Robert, her 85 year old groom, ready for action. They unite as one. All goes well, Robert takes leave of his bride, and she prepares to go to sleep.

After a few minutes, Jenny hears another knock on her bedroom door, and it's Robert, Again he is ready for more action. Somewhat surprised, Jenny consents for more coupling. When the newlyweds are done, Robert kisses his bride, bids her a fond good night and leaves.

She is set to go to sleep again, but, aha, you guessed it Robert is back again, rapping on the door and is as fresh as a 25 - year - old, ready for more 'action'. And, once more they enjoy each other.

But as Robert is about to leave again, his young bride says to him, "I'm thoroughly impressed that at your age you can perform so well and so often. I've been with guys less than a third of your age who were only good once. You are truly a great lover, Robert."

Robert, somewhat embarrassed, turns to Jenny and says, "You mean I was here already?"

MEMORY LOSS

A couple in their nineties are both having problems remembering things. During a check-up, the doctor tells them that they're physically okay, but they might want to write things down to help them remember.

Later that night, while watching TV, the old man gets up from his chair. "Want anything while I'm in the kitchen?" he asks.

"Will you get me a bowl of ice cream?"

"Sure."

"Don't you think you should write it down so you can remember it?" she asks.

"No, I can remember that."

"Well, I'd like some strawberries on top, too. Maybe you should write that down, so as not to forget it?"

He says, "I'll remember that. You want a bowl of ice cream with strawberries."

"I'd also like whipped cream. I'm certain you'll forget that, write it down?" she asks.

Irritated, he says, "I don't need to write it down, I can remember it! Ice cream with strawberries and whipped cream - for goodness sake!"

Then he toddles into the kitchen. After about 20 minutes, the old man returns from the kitchen and hands his wife a plate of bacon and eggs. She stares at the plate for a moment then asks, "Where's my toast?"

TRUE BLUE
AUSSIE FAMILIES

CAUGHT IN THE ACT

Tom was on his way to work when he realised that he didn't have his mobile phone with him. He pulled over and ran into a phone box to check if it was at home.

"Hello?" said a little girl's voice.

"Hi, honey, it's Daddy," said Tom. "Is Mummy there?"

"No, Daddy. She's upstairs with Uncle Drew."

After a brief pause, Tom said, "But you haven't got an Uncle Drew, sweetie!"

"Yes, I do, and he's upstairs in the bedroom with Mummy!"

"Okay, then. Put down the phone, run upstairs and knock on the bedroom door and shout in to Mummy and Uncle Drew that my car's just pulled up outside the house."

"Okay, Daddy!"

A few minutes later, the little girl came back to the phone. "Well, I did what you said, Daddy."

"And what happened?"

"Well, Mummy jumped out of bed with no clothes on and ran around screaming, then she tripped over the rug, fell out the front window and now she's not moving."

"Oh, my God! What about Uncle Drew?"

"He jumped out of bed with no clothes on too, and he was all scared and he jumped out the back window into the swimming pool. But he must have forgot that last week you took out all the water to clean it, so he hit the bottom and now he's not moving either."

There was a long pause.

"Swimming pool? Is this 9854 7039?"

THE BIG QUESTION

"Where did I come from, Mummy?' asked seven year old Robert. Mummy had been dreading this question but decided to be truthful. So she explained the sex act and then the pregnancy and then delivery at the local hospital.
She watched closely for his reaction.

"I just wondered," said Robert. "The boy who sits beside me at school came from New South Wales."

WWW DAD

A little boy goes up to his father and asks, "Daddy, how was I born?"
"Well, son," the father replies," your mum and I first got together in a chat room on the internet. I then set up a date via email with your mum and we met at a cyber café. We sneaked off into a secluded room and activated my hard drive. We then discovered that neither of us had used a firewall and it was too late to hit the delete button. Anyway, nine months later a blessed little pop-up appeared.
It read, 'You've got male'."

CIRCUMCISION

A teacher noticed that a little boy at the back of the class was squirming around, scratching his crotch and not paying attention.

"What's the matter Andrew?" she asked.

Andrew was quite embarrassed and whispered, "I've only just been circumcised the other day and it's itchy."

"Go down to the principal's office," the teacher instructed him. "Phone your mum, and ask her what you should do." Andrew did this and soon returned to the class and sat down in his seat. Suddenly, there was a great commotion at the back of the room. The teacher could see Andrew sitting at his desk with his penis hanging out.

"I thought I told you to call your mum," she said angrily.

"I did," he said. "She told me that if I could stick it out till noon, she'd come and pick me up from school."

LITTLE KATE

Once during the holidays, Janice took her four year old daughter Kate, with her to deliver Meals on Wheels to the elderly. Kate was intrigued by various appliances like canes, walkers and wheelchairs. But when she saw false teeth soaking in a glass she was fascinated. She observed in a loud voice, "The tooth fairy will never believe this!"

THE ELEVATOR

A family from the country were on their first visit to Sydney. The father and son were in the hotel lobby when they spotted an elevator.

"What's that, Pa?" the boy asked.

"I never did see nothin' like that in my life," replied his father.

Seconds later an old frail woman walked in the hotel door and hobbled to the elevator. She pressed the button with her walking stick, waited for the doors to open and got in.

The father and son, still amazed by this contraption, continued to watch. They heard a ping noise and the doors open again. Out stepped a beautiful young busty blonde.

The father grabbed his son by the shoulders and cried, "Quickly, go get your ma!"

LITTLE HELPER

A young family moved into a house next door to a vacant lot. One day a construction crew turned up to start building a house on the empty lot.

The young family's six-year-old daughter Sally naturally took an interest in all the activity going on next door and started talking with the workers. She hung around and eventually the construction crew – gems in the rough all of them – more or less adopted her as a kind of project mascot.

They chatted with Sally, let her sit with them while they had coffee and lunch breaks, and gave her little jobs to do here and there to make her feel important. At the end of the first week they even presented her with a pay envelope containing $5.

Sally took this home to her mother who said all the appropriate words of admiration and suggested that they take the pay she had received to the bank the next day to start a savings account.

When they got to the bank the teller was equally impressed with the story and asked the little girl how she had come by her very own pay cheque at such a young age. The little girl proudly replied, "I've been working with a crew building a house all week."

"My goodness gracious," said the teller, "and will you be working on the house again this week too?"

"I will if those useless bastards at the timber yard ever bring us the f***ing drywall," replied the little girl.

CURIOUS JANE

Three year old Jane was watching her mother breast-feeding her new baby brother. After a while Jane asked, "Mummy, why have you got two? Is one for hot milk and the other for cold?"

BOYS DAY OUT

A father walks into a restaurant with his young son. He gives the boy three coins to play with to keep him occupied.

Suddenly, the boy starts choking and going blue in the face. The father realises the boy has swallowed the coins and starts slapping him on the back.

The boy coughs up two of the coins, but keeps choking. The father panics and shouts for help.

An attractive, serious looking woman, in a blue business suit is sitting at a coffee bar reading a newspaper and sipping a cup of coffee. At the sound of the commotion, she looks up, puts her coffee cup down, neatly folds the newspaper and places it on the counter, gets up from her seat and makes her way, unhurriedly, across the restaurant.

Reaching the boy, the woman carefully drops his pants; takes hold of the boy's testicles and starts to squeeze and twist, gently at first and then ever so firmly.

After a few seconds the boy convulses violently and coughs up the last coin, which the woman deftly catches in her free hand. Releasing the boy's testicles, the woman hands the coin to the father and walks back to her seat at the coffee bar without saying a word.

As soon as he is sure that his son has suffered no ill effects, the father rushes over to the woman and thanks her saying, "I've never seen anybody do anything like that before, it was fantastic. Are you a doctor?"

"No," the woman replied: "I'm with the Tax Department."

HELP A BROTHER OUT

Two young boys walked into a pharmacy one day, picked out a box of tampons and went to the checkout counter. The pharmacist asked the older boy, "Son, how old are you?"

"Eight," the boy replied.

"Do you know what these are used for?"

The boy replied, "Not exactly, but they aren't for me. They're for him. He's my brother. He's four. We saw on TV that if you use these, you would be able to swim, play tennis and ride a bike. Right now, he can't do none of those."

AUNTY CHERYL

For homework a teacher told her class of 12 year olds to ask their parents to tell them a story with a moral at the end. The next day the kids came back and one by one began to tell their stories.

Karl said, "My father's a farmer and we have a lot of egg-laying chooks. One time we were taking our eggs to market in a basket on the front seat of the car when we hit a big bump in the road and all the eggs went flying and broke and made a mess." "What's the moral of the story?" asked the teacher.

"Don't put all your eggs in one basket!"

"Very good," said the teacher.

Next little Emily raised her hand and said, "Our family are farmers too. But we raise chooks for the meat market. One day we had a dozen eggs, but when they hatched we only got ten live chicks and the moral of this story is, 'Don't count your chickens before they're hatched.'"

"That was a fine story, Emily. Mick, do you have a story to share?"

"Yes. My dad told me this story about my Aunty Cheryl. Aunty Cheryl was a flight engineer on a plane in the Gulf War and her plane got hit. She had to bail out over enemy territory and all she had was three bottles of rum, a machine gun and a machete. She drank all the rum on the way down so it wouldn't break and then she landed right in the middle of 100 enemy troops. She killed seventy of them with the machine gun until she ran out of bullets. Then she killed twenty more with the machete until the blade broke. And then she killed the last ten with her bare hands."

"Good heavens," said the horrified teacher, "what kind of moral did your father tell you from that horrible story?"

"Stay right away from Aunty Cheryl when she's been on the grog!"

FOLLOWING SUIT

A little boy was watching his parents dress for a party. When he saw his dad donning his dinner jacket, he warned,
"Daddy, you shouldn't wear that suit."

"Why not Tim?"

"It always gives you a headache the next morning."

HELLO-COPPER

The boss of a new employee needs to call him at home about an urgent problem with one of the main computers. After dialing he's greeted by a child's whisper, "Hello."

"Is your daddy home?" he asked.

"Yes," whispered the small voice.

"May I talk with him?"

"No," whispers the child.

Surprised, the boss asked, "Is your mummy there?"

"Yes."

"May I talk with her?"

Again the small voice whispered, "No."

Hoping there was somebody with whom he could leave a message, the boss asked, "Is anyone else there?"

"Yes," whispered the child, "a policeman."

Wondering what was going on the boss asked, "May I speak with the policeman?"

"No, he's busy," whispered the child.

"Busy doing what?"

"Talking to Mummy and Daddy and the fireman," came the whispered answer. Growing worried as he heard what sounded like a helicopter, the boss asked,

"What's going on?" the boss asked alarmed.

In an awed whisper the child answered, "The search team just landed the hello-copper." Really worried now, the boss asked, "What are they searching for?"

"Me!"

BURIED BODIES

An old retired old man wanted to plant his annual tomato garden, but it was very difficult work. His only son, Vincent, who used to help him, was in prison. The old man wrote a letter to his son and described his predicament:

Dear Vincent,

I am feeling pretty sad, because it looks like I won't be able to plant my tomato garden this year. I'm just getting too old to be digging up a garden plot. I know if you were here my troubles would be over. I know you would be happy to dig the plot for me, like in the old days.

Love, Papa.

A few days later he received a letter from his son.

Dear Pop,

Don't dig up that garden. That's where the bodies are buried.

Love, Vinnie.

At 4 am the next morning, the police arrived and dug up the entire area, but without finding any bodies. They apologised to the old man and left. The next day the old man received another letter.

Dear Pop,

Go ahead and plant the tomatoes now. That's the best I could do under the circumstances. Love you, Vinnie.

THE BIRDS AND THE BEES

Wendy asked her ten-year-old son if he knew about the birds and the bees.

"I don't want to know!" Roger cried out, bursting into tears. "Promise me you won't tell me."

Confused, Wendy asked him what was wrong.

"Oh Mum," the boy sobbed, "When I was seven I got the 'there's no Santa' speech. At eight, I got the 'There's no Easter Bunny' speech. When I was nine, you hit me with the 'There's no Tooth Fairy' speech. If you tell me that grown-ups don't really f★★★, I'll have nothing left to live for."

BABIES

With all the advances in modern medicine, a 67-year-old friend of mine was able to give birth. When she was discharged from the hospital and went home, I paid a visit.

"May I see the new baby?" I asked.

"Not yet," she said. "I'll make coffee and we can chat first."

Half an hour passed, and I asked, "May I see the bub now?"

"No, not yet," she said. After another while, I asked again.

"No, not yet," replied my friend. Growing very impatient, I asked, 'Well, when can I see the baby?'

"When he cries!" she said.

"When he cries?" I said. "Why?"

"BECAUSE I FORGOT WHERE I PUT HIM, OK?"

FAMILY DINNER

Several family friends met regularly at each other's homes for dinner and then to play cards. When it was Frank and Jenny's turn to host, Jenny decided on a mushroom and chicken pie. Frank suggested she pick the mushrooms in the paddock at the back of their house. Jenny was a bit worried that they might be poisonous. But Frank reminded her that their dog Red ate them and he was okay.

So Jenny decided to give it a try. She picked some and washed, sliced, and diced them for her pie. Then she gave Red some left overs and he wolfed them down. After the meal, which was a great success they settled down to a card game of 500. But a few minutes later the front door bell rang and on Jenny opening the door, the neighbour rushed in crying out, "Red is dead!"

Jenny became hysterical. What was going to happen to her guests and Frank and herself? After she finally calmed down, she called the doctor and told him what had happened. The doctor said, "Stay calm. I'll call an ambulance and come as soon as I can. Everything will be fine."

The ambulance soon arrived. The officers and doctor took each person into the bathroom, gave them an enema, and pumped out their stomach.

After they finished, the doctor said, "Everyone should be fine now," and left. They were all feeling weak and slouched on the living room arm chairs when the neighbour whispered to Jenny, "You know, that driver who ran over Red didn't even stop."

BOYS WILL BE BOYS

Two boys, ages 8 and 10, were very mischievous and were always getting into trouble. If any mischief occurred in their town, the two boys were probably involved.

The boys' mother heard that a local minister was good at disciplining children, so she asked him to speak with her boys.

The minister agreed and asked to see them individually. So the mother sent the eight year old in the morning to be followed by the older boy in the afternoon. The minister, a huge man with a booming voice, sat the younger boy down and asked him sternly, "Do you know where God is, son?" The boy's mouth dropped open, but he made no response, sitting there wide-eyed with his mouth hanging open.

So the minister repeated the question in an even sterner tone, "Where is God?" Again, the boy made no attempt to answer.

The minister raised his voice even more and shook his finger in the boy's face and bellowed, "Where is God?"

The boy screamed and bolted from the room, ran directly home and dove into his cupboard, slamming the door behind him. When his older brother found him, he asked, "What happened?"

The younger brother, gasping for breath, replied, "We're in BIG trouble this time. GOD is missing, and they think we did it!"

MISSED OUT

It was Palm Sunday and because of a cold, six year old Tim stayed at home with his dad while his mum and sister Ella went to church. When the family returned they were carrying several palm branches. Tim asked what they were for.

"People placed them on the road for Jesus and his donkey to ride over," Ella said. "Crumbs! The one Sunday I don't go, he shows up!"

QUIZ MASTER

Don is on a quiz show. To the surprise of his family and friends he hangs in to the last question.

Quiz Master: "This is the million dollar question. You ready?"

Don: "Yes."

Quiz Master: "Which of the following birds does not build its own nest? Is it A) robin, B) sparrow, C) cuckoo?"

Don: "That's simple. It's a cuckoo."

Quiz Master: "Are you sure?"

Don: "I'm sure."

Quiz Master: "You said C) cuckoo, and you're right! Congratulations, you have just won one million dollars!"

To celebrate, Don takes his girlfriend Cheryl to Hawaii. Over dinner she says, "I had no idea you were so clever Don. How did you know it was the cuckoo that didn't build its own nest?"

"That's easy - they live in clocks."

LETTERS FROM GRANDMA

Grandma is ninety years old and still drives her own car. She writes to her granddaughter.

Dear Jeannette,

The other day I went to our local Christian book store and saw a 'Honk if you love Jesus' bumper sticker.

I was feeling particularly upbeat because I'd just been to an inspiring prayer meeting.

So, I bought the sticker and put it on my bumper.

I'm so glad I did! What an uplifting experience followed.

I had stopped at a red light at a busy intersection, lost in thought about the Lord and how good he is, and I didn't notice that the light had changed.

It's a good thing someone else loves Jesus because if he hadn't honked, I'd never have noticed.

I found that lots of people love Jesus! While I was sitting there, the man behind me started honking like crazy, and then he leaned out of his window and screamed, "For the love of God! Go! Go! Go!"

What an exuberant cheerleader he was for Jesus! Everyone started honking!

I leaned out my window and started waving and smiling at all those loving people.

I even honked my horn a few times to share in the love!

I saw one man waving in a funny way with only his middle finger stuck up in the air. I asked your cousin, Johnny, who was in the back seat what that meant.

He said it was probably a good luck sign. What a lovely thought. So I leaned out the window and gave him the good luck sign right back. *Johnny burst out laughing. Even he was enjoying this religious experience!*

A couple of the people were so caught up in the joy of the moment that they got out of their cars and started walking towards me.

I bet they wanted to pray or ask what church I attended, but this is when I noticed the light had changed.

So, grinning, I waved at all my brothers and sisters, and drove on through the intersection.

I noticed that I was the only car that got through the intersection before the light changed again and felt sorry that I had to leave them after all the love we had shared. So I slowed the car down, leaned out the window and gave them all the good luck sign one last time as I drove away. Praise the Lord for such wonderful people!

Will write again soon.

Love,

Grandma

THANKS, MUM

A young man shopping in a supermarket noticed a little old lady following him around. If he stopped, she stopped. And she kept staring at him. She finally overtook him at the checkout, and turned to him saying, "I hope I haven't made you feel ill at ease; it's just that you look so much like my late son."

He answered, "That's alright."

"I know it's silly, but if you'd call out 'Goodbye, Mum' as I leave the store, it would make me feel so happy."

She then went through the checkout, and as she was on her way out of the store, the man called out, "Goodbye, Mum."

The little old lady waved and smiled back at him. Pleased that he had brought a little sunshine into someone's day, the young man went to pay for his groceries.

"That comes to $121.85," said the cashier. "How come it's so much? I only bought five items."

The cashier replied, "Yeah, but your mother said you'd pay for her things, too.

MOTHERS

Our mother taught us RELIGION: "You'd better pray that comes out of the carpet."

Our mother taught us LOGIC: "If you fall out of that swing and break your neck, you're not going to the shops with me."

Our mother taught us FORESIGHT: "Make sure you wear clean underwear in case you're hit by a bus."

Our mother taught us IRONY: "Keep crying and I'll give you something to cry about."

Our mother taught us about STAMINA: "You'll sit there until all that spinach is finished."

Our mother taught us about WEATHER: "It looks like a tornado has been through your room."

Our mother taught us about JUSTICE: "One day you'll have kids and I hope they turn out just like you!"

Our mother taught us about ANTICIPATION: "Just wait until your father gets home."

MAMA KNOWS BEST

Mrs Ravioli visits her son Tony for dinner. He lives with a female flatmate, Maria.

During the course of the meal, Mrs Ravioli notices how pretty Maria is. As the evening goes on she watches Tony and Maria interact and starts to wonder if there is more between Tony and his flatmate than meets the eye. Reading his mother's thoughts, Tony volunteers, "I know what you must be thinking, but I assure you, Maria and I are just flatmates."

About a week later, Maria came to Tony saying, "Ever since your mother came to dinner, I've been unable to find the silver sugar bowl. You don't suppose she took it, do you?"

"Well, I doubt it, but I'll email her, just to be sure."

He wrote:

Dear Mama,

I'm not saying that you 'took' the sugar bowl from my house. I'm not saying that you 'didn't take' it. But it's been missing ever since you were here for dinner. Your Loving Son, Tony.

Several days later, Tony received a response email from his mother which read:

Dear son,

I'm not saying that you 'do' sleep with Maria, and I'm not saying that you 'do not' sleep with her.

But the fact remains that if she was sleeping in her OWN bed, she would have found the sugar bowl by now.

Your Loving Mama.

PERKS OF BEING OVER 75

Kidnappers are not very interested in you.

In a hostage situation you're likely to be released first.

No one expects you to run - anywhere.

People call at 9 pm and ask, "Did I wake you?"

People no longer view you as a hypochondriac.

There's nothing left to learn the hard way.

Things you buy now won't wear out.

You can eat dinner at 4 pm.

You can live without sex but not your glasses.

You get into heated arguments about pension plans.

You no longer think of speed limits as a challenge.

You quit trying to hold your stomach in no matter who walks into the room.

You sing along with elevator music.

Your eyes won't get much worse.

Your investment in health insurance is finally beginning to pay off.

Your joints are more accurate meteorologists than the national weather service.

Your secrets are safe with your friends because they can't remember them either.

Your supply of brain cells is finally down to manageable size.

THIRSTY

A small boy is sent to bed by his father.

Five minutes later: "Da-ad..."

"What?"

"I'm thirsty. Can you bring a drink of water?"

"No. You had your chance. Lights out."

Five minutes later: "Da-aaaad......"

"WHAT?"

"I'm THIRSTY. Can I have a drink of water?"

"I told you NO! If you ask again, I'll have to smack you!!"

Five minutes later: "Daaaa-aaaad..."

"WHAT!"

"When you come in to smack me, can you bring a drink of water?"

THE GOAT

The young couple invited their elderly pastor for Sunday dinner.

While they were in the kitchen preparing the meal, the minister asked their five year old son what they were having.

"Goat," the little boy replied.

"Goat?" replied the startled man of the cloth, "Are you sure about that?"

"Yes," said the youngster. "I heard Daddy say to Mummy, 'Today is just as good as any to have the old goat for dinner.'"

YOUNG JEANNETTE

Four-year-old Jeannette asked her mother if she could play outside with the boys next door.

Mum said, "No you can't play with the boys. They're too rough."

Jeanette thought about this for a while then asked, "If I can find a smooth one, can I play with him?"

PARENTHOOD

A single mother fills in a child support document at Centrelink and says she has 12 children. She notes their names: the oldest is Peter, next is Peter, next is a girl called Peta, and the next two are called Peta, then the next is a boy called Peter and so on. The clerk notes this and says, "Ah I see a pattern here. Do you have any children who are not called Peter or Peta?"

"No," says the woman all the boys are called Peter and all the girls, Peta."

"Why have you done this?" asks the clerk.

"It's very handy," says the mother. "When I want them to get up I just call out one name or if I want them to come to dinner or to go and catch the bus to school and so on."

"But what if you just wanted to speak to one child?" asked the clerk.

"Oh then I call them by their surname," said the mother.

MEET YA
AT THE PUB!

STRONG MAN

Three guys were talking in the local bar. The manager was so sure that its bouncer was the strongest man around that it ordered a standing $1,000 bet that no one could beat him.

The challenge was that the bouncer would squeeze a lemon until all the juice ran out into a beer glass, then hand the lemon to the customer. Anyone who could squeeze even one more drop out of the lemon would win the money.

Over the years many people had tried this, truck drivers, weightlifters, karate masters, and all had failed. Then one day this geeky little fella with heavy black rimmed glasses came into the bar and asked if he could try the challenge. After the laughter had subsided the manager said that it was only fair that the man be given a chance at the bet, so the bouncer picked up a lemon and started squeezing. Once he was done he handed the remains to the little man who promptly squeezed out four more drops of juice onto the bar!

THREE WISE MEN

Three old men are out walking.
Don says, "Windy, isn't it?"
Ted replies, "No, it's Thursday!"
Pete says, "So am I. Let's get a beer."

PUBLIC TRANSPORT

Last night I was out with me mates and had way too much beer. Knowing I was drunk, I did something I'd never done before. I took a bus home. I arrived home safely and I was really pleased, 'cause I'd never driven a bus before!

OLD TIMER

Reginald was in a bar and noticed an old guy, about 80 years old, sitting all alone in the corner. He was crying into his cocktail. Reg went up to the man and asked him what was wrong.

The old fellow told him, "I have a 20 year old lover at home. I met her a month or so ago, right here in this very bar. She makes love to me every morning and then she makes me pancakes, sausage, fresh fruit and freshly ground, brewed coffee."

Reg was puzzled. "Well, then why are you crying?"

The old man continued, "She makes me homemade soup for lunch and my favourite brownies and then she makes love to me half the afternoon."

"Well, so why are you crying?" Reg persisted.

"For dinner she makes me a gourmet meal with wine and my favorite dessert and then she makes love to me until 2 am."

Reg was perplexed. "Well, for goodness sake! Why in the world would you be crying!" he shouted.

The old man cried out "I can't bloody remember where I live!"

FAMILY INHERITANCE

Dan was a single guy living at home with his father and working in the family business.

When he found out he was going to inherit a fortune when his elderly father died, he decided he needed to find a wife with whom to share his fortune.

One evening, at an investment meeting, he spotted the most beautiful woman he'd ever seen. She took his breath away.

"I may look like an ordinary guy," he said to her. "But in a few years my father will die and I will inherit $200 million."

Impressed, the woman asked for his business card and one week later, she became his stepmother.

SECRETS OF STAYING ALIVE

Three grey-haired guys went into the local pub.
The barman asked the first guy, "What age are you, mate?"

"81, and it's because of milk. Milk in the morning, milk in the afternoon and milk at night," he said.

"That's great," said the barman. He turned to the second bloke. "What age are you?"

"I'm 82," he said, "and it's beer, beer in the morning, beer in the afternoon and beer at night."

"Even better," said the barman. He looked at the third guy, and asked, "What's your secret?"

"Women. Women in the morning, women in the afternoon and women at night," he said.

"Brilliant!" said the barman. "And how old are you?"

"If I live to next Friday, I'll be 22."

Everyone looked on in amazement as the landlord handed over the prize and asked, "What do you do for a living that has given you such strength? Are you a lumberjack, weightlifter, what?"

"No," the man replied, "I work for the tax office."

FESTIVITIES

Three mates were enjoying a Christmas Eve drink together at the local pub. It was around 10 p.m. when one of them remembered that a friend of his was holding a party down the road. When they arrived, the host said, "You have to show something that symbolises Christmas."

Jake rummaged in his pockets and pulled out his bunch of keys. "They're bells," he said.

"Good one," said the host.

Bert took out a box of matches. He lit one and said, "It's a candle."

"Fine," said the host.

Frank rummaged in his back pockets and pulled out a panty.

"What's that supposed to symbolise?" asked the host.

"They're Carol's," Frank replied.

REVENGE

Five Hell's Angels bikers walked into a pub, ordered beers and told the lone drinker at the end of the bar to pay. When he refused they punched him up and threw him out of the pub.

"He wasn't much of a fighter," said one of the bikies to the barman.

"He's not much of a driver, either," said the barman.

"He's just driven his truck over five motorbikes."

PRIEST'S COLLAR

A drunk was sitting opposite a priest on the bus, he studied him for a while and finally said, "Tell me, yer worship. Why do you wear your collar back to front?"

"Because I'm a father," said the priest.

"But I'm a father too," said the drunk.

"No I'm a father to hundreds in my parish."

"Then maybe it's your trousers you should be wearing back to front," said the drunk.

FIRE ALARM

Brian and Max were sitting in the pub having a beer when the town's fire alarm started to ring. Max jumped up and headed for the door.

Brian called out, "I didn't know you were a fireman."

"I'm not," Max said. "But my girlfriend's husband is."

NUNS' REMEDY

A nun went into the local and asked for a bottle of whiskey.

"Whiskey?" the barman asked, "I thought you nuns didn't drink."

"We don't," the nun replied, "this is for the Mother Superior's constipation."

She bought the whiskey and left.

Later that night, the barman saw the same nun dead drunk on a park bench. "I thought that was for the Mother Superior's constipation?"

"It ish," the nun replied. "When she sees me like this, she'll sh★★ herself!"

TOO MUCH TO DRINK

A drunk staggered into the reception area of the Shepparton Hotel and said to the desk clerk, "I'd like the key to room 607, please."

"I'm sorry, sir," said the clerk. "That room is occupied."
"Not now it isn't," replied the drunk. "I just fell out of the window."

FORGOT SOMETHING?

A man was at a pub drinking all night.

When the barman called out that the pub was closing, the man stood up to leave and fell flat on his face.

He tried to stand again, but ended up face down again.

He figured he needed some fresh air so he crawled outside.

Once outside he tried to stand again, with the same result.

He made up his mind to crawl the four blocks home. When he reached the door he stood up and fell straight down again. He crawled through the door into his bedroom.

When he reached his bed he tried one last time to stand up. This time he managed to pull himself upright but quickly fell into bed and was asleep as soon as his head hit the pillow.

He woke the following morning to find his wife standing over him.

"So, you've been out drinking again!" she shouted at him.

"What makes you say that?" he asked, smiling innocently.

"The pub called... you left your wheelchair there again."

SHORT CHANGED

There were three men drinking in a bar.

After they drank a lot of beers they were about to leave, but found they were $12 short of the tab. The owner of the bar came out to see them.

"Because you're short of the money and I'm a generous man, I will let this go if you have twelve inches of dick between you. One inch for each dollar you owe," he told them.

The first guy whipped his out and showed six inches.

The second guy dropped his pants and showed five inches.

Finally, the third guy showed his one inch dick. The barman

said "Okay, that's twelve inches. You can go".

As they were walking away the first guy said to the third, "Thank God you managed to get a stiffy too, or we'd still be there."

HORSING AROUND

A bloke went into a pub, sat down and ordered a gin.
The barman gave him one, and the man noticed a horse at the end of the bar. He asked the bartender why there was a horse standing at the bar.

"I'll show you," the barman replied. He picked up a cricket bat and hit the horse over the head. The horse gave the barman a blow-job.

"Wow! I've never seen anything like it!"

"You want a go?" asked the barman.

"Sure, but there's no need to hit me over the head!"

DRINKING IS A SIN

John was sitting outside his local pub one day, enjoying a quiet pint and generally feeling good about himself, when a nun suddenly appeared at his table and started decrying the evils of drink.

"You should be ashamed of yourself young man! Drinking is a sin! Alcohol is the blood of the devil!"

Now John became pretty annoyed about this, and went on the offensive.

"How do you know this, Sister?"

"My Mother Superior told me so."

"But have you ever had a drink yourself? How can you be sure that what you are saying is correct?"

"Don't be ridiculous – of course I have never taken alcohol myself."

"Then let me buy you a drink – if you still believe afterwards that it is evil I will give up drink for life."

"How could I – a nun – sit outside this public house drinking?!"

"I'll get the barman to put it in a teacup for you so no one will ever know."

The nun reluctantly agreed, so John went inside to the bar.

"Another pint for me, and a triple vodka on the rocks," then he lowered his voice and said to the barman, "and could you put the vodka in a teacup?"

"Oh no! It's not that nun again is it?"

PATTY'S PROBLEM

Patrick, a lapsed Catholic is stricken with guilt and unwillingly feels he had better go to confession so that he can start a new life.

He enters the confessional cubicle and is amazed at how things have changed since he was last there. There's a bar with wine, champagne and liqueurs. Beside it is a shelf filled with cigars and chocolates. The door opens and in comes Father O'Farrell.

"Father, please forgive me for not coming to confession all

these years," says Patrick. "My, how things have changed. The confessional is so much more inviting than when I was last here," he said.

Father O'Farrell responds: "Get out. This is my side."

TECHNOLOGY

One day, at the pub, Bob says to Jack, "The local supermarket has just installed a diagnostic computer. For only $10 you just have to give it a urine sample and the computer will tell you what's wrong and what to do about it. You don't have to pay steep doctor's bills."

As it happened Jack had a sore wrist that kept him awake at nights. So he thought he'd give it a try.

So Jack deposits a urine sample in a small jar and takes it to the supermarket.

He pays $10 and the computer lights up and asks for the urine sample. He pours the sample into the slot and waits.

A few seconds later, the computer spits out a printout:

You have a strained tendon.

Soak your wrist in warm water twice daily, avoid activity and it will improve in two weeks.

After one week his wrist had improved, although it was still sore. He was so impressed with the computer, but he wondered if it could be fooled.

So Jack mixed a stool sample from his cat, urine samples from his wife and son and a sperm sample from himself.

Jack went back to the Supermarket computer, deposited the

$10 and poured in the mixture.

A few moments later the computer ejects a paper slip saying:

1. *Your cat has ringworm. Bathe her with anti-fungal shampoo (aisle two).*
2. *Your son is addicted to heroine. Take him to a rehab clinic.*
3. *Your wife is pregnant. Not yours. Find a lawyer.*
4. *Stop playing with yourself, or your wrist will not recover.*

FRED'S SHOUT

Fred was sitting at the bar staring at his drink when a large, aggressive bikie grabbed his drink and swigged it down...

He stared at Fred with his hands on his hips and said, "Well, whatcha' gonna do about it?"

Then Fred burst into tears.

"Hey Man," the bikie said, "Wacha doin'? I can't stand seein' a man cryin'."

"This is the worst day of my life," Fred said. "I'm a total failure. My boss fired me. Then my car was stolen from the work car park and I don't have any insurance. I left my wallet in the taxi I took home. There I found my wife in bed with my best friend and then my dog bit me.

"So I came here to get the courage to end it all. I buy a drink, I drop a tablet in it and watch the poison dissolve; then you show up and drink the whole thing! But enough about me, how're you going?"

A WISE WINO

A wine shop's regular taster moved to France to improve his skills. The owner advertised the position. Months passed but he couldn't find anyone with the necessary expertise.

One day a drunk in dirty clothes arrives for an interview. The owner wonders how he could get rid of him. He gives him a glass to taste.

The drunk sips the wine and correctly recognizes that the drink is a cabernet two years old, grown on a southern slope, matured in steel containers, of ordinary grade, but adequate.

Obviously this drunk knows something, thinks the owner.

So he tests him on another wine.

"This is a Sauvignon Blanc, six years of age, grown on a north western slope, matured in oak barrels and requires four more years for best results."

"Hmm" thinks the owner, "It's not going to be so easy to get rid of him."

He gives the drunk another glass to try. Again, he's spot on.

"This is a Pinot Noir and a rare fine grade," he says.

The owner is impressed, but he still doesn't want to employ this man. So he thinks of a test that the drunk would be sure to fail.

He whispers to his red-haired secretary, who promptly leaves the room and soon returns with a glass of urine.

The drunk tries it and spits it out. "It's a 20 year old red-head, four months pregnant - and if I don't get this job, I'll name the father."

LITTLE GUY

A small man was quietly sipping a beer in a pub when a large man approached him and hit him hard in the face.

The large man said, "That's Kung Fu from China."

The little man was too stunned to speak.

Then a few minutes later while the little man was still recovering, the large man approached him again and whacked him again in the face saying, "That's Judo from Japan."

The little man was astonished.

After awhile he left the bar and some time later returned. He went up to the large man who was still drinking at the bar, and gave him a whack on the face knocking him out.

The little man said to the bartender, "When he wakes up tell him, that was a shovel from Bunnings."

LONELY

A lonely guy decides to buy a pet to bring more fun to his life. So he goes to the pet shop and asks the owner for an unusual pet. After some discussion he buys a centipede, which comes in a little white box to use for his house.

He takes the box home and decides he will start by taking his new pet to the bar for a drink. So he asks the centipede in the box, "Would you like to go to the local pub with me and have a beer?" But there is no answer from his new pet. This bothers him a bit, so he waits a few minutes and then asks again, "How about going to the bar and having a drink with me?"

Again there is no answer from his new friend and pet. He decides to ask him one more time. This time putting his face up against the centipede's house and shouting, "Hey, in there! Would you like to go to the local pub and have a drink with me?"

Then he hears a little voice from the box, "I heard you the

first time! I'm just putting my shoes on!"

COPPAS & POLITICS

EMBARRASSED

The Prime Minister was walking by the lake in Canberra and, preoccupied by affairs of state, slipped and fell in.

A young lad heard his cries for help and dived in and saved him. When he recovered the Prime Minister said to the lad, "You saved my life. Anything you can name you can have."

"I don't want anything," said the youth. "Just don't tell my dad. He didn't vote for you."

JUST LIKE A POLITICIAN

A member of parliament decided to take up ballooning.

On his first trip, the weather took a turn for the worse and the balloon was forced down into a paddock miles from anywhere.

Just then he noticed a farmer crossing the paddock and shouted, "Could you please tell me where I am?"

"You're in a balloon!" the farmer shouted back, and carried on walking.

Recounting this incident to his colleagues in a Canberra pub the next day, the MP said, "That farmer gave me the perfect politicians reply. It was short. It was true. And it gave absolutely no new information."

STOLEN CAR

A drunk phoned police to report that thieves had been in his car.

"They've stolen the dashboard, the steering wheel, the brake pedal, even the accelerator!" he cried out.

However, before the police investigation could start, the phone rang a second time and the same voice came over the line.

"Never mind," he said with a hiccup, "I got in the back seat by mistake."

BORDER SECURITY

Did you hear about the Englishman who was stopped by Australian immigration officers at Sydney airport? They asked him if he had a criminal record. He replied, "I didn't know it was still necessary."

PASSED AWAY

A man telephoned his lawyer's office. When the receptionist answered the phone he asked to speak to Mr Smyth, his lawyer.

The receptionist replied, "I'm sorry, but Mr Smyth died last week." The man said nothing and hung up the phone.

The next day he called the office and again asked for Mr Smyth.

The receptionist said, "Sir, I told you yesterday that Mr Smyth has died." The man again said nothing and hung up the phone.

The next day he called the office again and asked for his lawyer. The receptionist became angry and said "Sir, I have told you for two days that Mr Smyth has passed away. Why do you continue to call?"

The man explained, "I like hearing good news when I call my lawyer's office."

4AM LECTURE

A man around 40 is running along the main street at around 4 a.m. He is stopped by a policeman who asks him what he's doing up at this time of night. The man replies, "I'm on my way to a lecture about gambling, alcohol abuse and staying out late." The policeman asks, "Who'd give such a lecture at this time?" "My wife," the man replies.

CAUGHT OUT

A young lawyer had just gone into practice.

He had been sitting at his desk a week when he saw a man come into his outer office. Quickly he picked up his phone and pretended to be negotiating a big deal.

He spoke loudly about large sums of money and possible court proceedings. When he hung up he looked at the visitor and said, "Can I help you?"

"Yes," said the man. "I've come to connect your phone."

SPEED MACHINE

A mature woman is pulled over for speeding.

Woman: "Is there a problem, officer?"

Officer: "Madam, you were speeding."

Woman: "Oh, I see."

Officer: "Can I see your licence please?"

Woman: "I'd give it to you but I don't have one."

Officer: "You don't have one?!"

Woman: "I lost it, four years ago for drunk driving."

Officer: "Can I see your vehicle registration papers please?"

Woman: "I can't do that."

Officer: "Why not?"

Woman: "I stole this car."

Officer: "Stole it?"

Woman: "Yes, and I killed and hacked up the owner."

Officer: "You what?"

Woman: "His body parts are in plastic bags in the trunk if you want to see."

The officer looks at the woman and slowly backs away to his car and calls for back up. Within minutes three police cars circle the car. A senior officer slowly approaches the car, clasping his half-drawn gun.

Senior officer: "Madam, could you step out of your vehicle please!" The woman does so.

Woman: "Is there a problem, sir?"

Senior officer: "One of my officers told me that you stole this car and murdered the owner."

Woman: "Murdered the owner?"

Senior officer: "Yes, could you open the trunk of your car, please?"

The woman opens the trunk, revealing nothing but an empty trunk.

Senior officer: "Is this your car, madam?"

Woman: "Yes, here are the registration papers."

The officer is stunned.

Senior officer: "My officer claims that you don't have a driving licence."

The woman digs into her handbag and pulls out a clutch purse and hands it to the officer.

The officer examines the licence and looks quite puzzled.

Senior officer: "Thank you, madam, my officer told me you didn't have a licence, that you stole this car, and that you murdered and hacked up the owner."

Woman: "Bet the liar told you I was speeding, too!"

TONY ON TOUR

Malcolm Turnbull is visiting the UK and is impressed by the charisma of the royal family so he asks the Queen for the secret.

She replies that she keeps them on their toes by asking challenging questions.

The Duke of Edinburgh passes by and the Queen asks, "Phillip if your mother had a child but it isn't your brother or your sister, who is it ?"

Phillip says, "That's easy. It's me."

"Correct," says the Queen. Malcolm is impressed.

Back in Australia, Malcolm tries this with the treasurer Joe Hockey.

"Joe, if your mother has a child but it is not your brother or your sister, who is it?"

Joe is puzzled, so says he will ask the smartest parliamentarian, Clive Palmer.

"Clive, your mother has a child but it is not your brother or your sister, who is it?" Clive replies, "I'm glad you've asked me for guidance Joe, of course the answer is me."

Joe scuttles back to Malcolm. "Malcolm I have the answer to that brother and sister poser, the answer is Clive Palmer!"

Malcolm sarcastically replies, "We mustn't let the electorate know Joe, but you're a moron. It's obvious that the answer is the Duke of Edinburgh."

ST PETER AND THE POLITICIAN

While crossing the road, a well-known politician is hit by a dunny truck and dies. His soul arrives in heaven, and he is met by St Peter.

"Welcome," says St Peter. "Unfortunately there's a slight problem. We seldom see politicians up here, so we're not sure what to do with you."

"No problem," says the politician, "just let me in."

"I'd like to, but I have orders from 'on high.' You need to spend a day in hell, and a day in heaven. Then you can choose where to spend eternity."

"Oh no need, I want to be in heaven," says the politician. "I'm sorry but rules are rules," insists St Peter. And with that, St. Peter escorts the politician to the lift which takes him down to hell. The doors open and he finds himself in the middle of a green golf course. In the distance is a club, and standing in front of it are all his friends and other politicians who'd worked with him. Everyone is happy and they run to greet him, shake his hand, and reminisce about the good times. They play a great game of golf and then dine on crayfish, caviar and champagne. Also present is the devil, who's very friendly and funny. They're all having such a good time that, before he realises, it's time to go. Everyone gives the politician a hearty farewell and wave while the lift takes him on its upward journey. It goes all the way to heaven, where St Peter is waiting.

"Now it's time for you to visit heaven." So the pollie joins a group of contented souls, moving from cloud to cloud playing the harp and, before he realises it, the 24 hours have gone by, and St. Peter returns.

"You've spent a day in hell and a day in heaven. Now choose for eternity."

The politician reflects for a minute, then answers, "Well heaven has been delightful, but I'm surprised to say that I'd be better off in hell." So, St Peter escorts him to the lift and the politician goes down, down, down to hell.

The lift doors open, and he finds he's in the middle of a barren land covered with waste and debris. He sees all his friends, but this time dressed in rags, picking up rubbish and putting it in bags. The Devil comes over to him and puts his arm around his shoulder.

"I don't understand," stammers the pollie. "Yesterday there was a golf course and a club, we ate crayfish and caviar, drank champagne and had a great time. Now there's nothing but a wasteland full of garbage, and my friends look miserable. What happened?"

The Devil looks at him, smiles and says, "Yesterday we were campaigning; today you voted..."

A CHEEKY CELEBRATION

A woman and a man are involved in a car accident. It's a bad one. Both of their cars are totally demolished but amazingly neither of them are hurt.

After they crawl out of their cars, the woman says, "Wow, look at our cars! There's nothing left but fortunately we're not hurt. This must be a sign from God that we should be friends and be at peace with one another."

The man replied, "I agree with you completely. This must be a sign from God!"

The woman continued, "And look, here's another miracle. My car is completely demolished but this bottle of wine didn't break. Surely God wants us to drink this wine and celebrate our good fortune."

Then she hands the bottle to the man. The man shakes his head in agreement, opens it and drinks half the bottle and then hands it back to the woman.

The woman takes the bottle, immediately puts the cap back on, and hands it back to the man.

The man asks, "Aren't you having any?"

The woman replies, "No, I think I'll just wait for the police…"

FARMER JOHN

Farmer John lived on a quiet rural highway west of Geelong. As time went by, the traffic increased in the area. The traffic got so heavy and so fast that Farmer John's free range chickens were being run over at a rate of three to six a day.

So John called the local policeman to complain.

"You've got to do something about all these people driving so fast and killing my chickens."

"What do you want me to do?" asked the policeman.

"I don't care. Just do something about those crazy drivers!"

So the next day the policeman asked the council to put up a sign that said: SLOW: SCHOOL CROSSING.

Three days later Farmer John called the policeman and said, "You've still got to do something about these drivers. The school crossing sign doesn't make any difference!"

So this time, the policeman asked the council to put up a new sign: SLOW: CHILDREN AT PLAY. That didn't make any difference either. So Farmer John called and called every day for three weeks. Finally, he said to the policeman "Your signs are no good. Can I put up my own?"

'Anything to get him off my back', thought the policeman, so he agreed.

He then got no more calls from Farmer John.

Three weeks later, curiosity got the better of the policeman so he gave Farmer John a call.

"How's the problem with those drivers. Did you put up your sign?"

"I sure did," replied Farmer John, "and not one chicken has been killed since then. I've got to go. I'm very busy."

The policeman was really curious now and decided to see the sign for himself. Perhaps it might be something the police could use to slow down traffic elsewhere.

So he drove to John's farm and his jaw dropped the moment he saw the sign. It was spray painted on a sheet of plywood... 'NUDIST COLONY - Slow down and watch out for chicks!'

THE PERFECT ROBBERY

A pair of lovers, Samuel and Carl, fell on hard times and decided to rob a bank together. Samuel plotted the robbery and then instructed Carl with the plan in great detail. The only problem was that Carl couldn't drive, so he had to be the one inside the bank.

The next week when they drove up in front of the bank, Samuel asked Carl, "I want to make absolutely sure you understand the plan. You are supposed to be in and out of the bank in less than three minutes with the cash.

Do you understand the plan?"

"Perfectly," he said.

Carl went into the bank while Samuel waited nervously in the getaway van. One minute passed, two minutes passed... by the time seven minutes had passed, Samuel was really worried.

Finally, the bank doors burst open and Carl came out. He had a rope wrapped around the safe and dragged it slowly towards the van. After he had got it in the van, the bank doors burst open again and the security guard stumbled out with his pants and underwear down around his ankles, firing his gun at the robbers.

As they were speeding away, Samuel said to Carl, "I thought you understood the plan!"

Carl replied angrily, "I did! I did exactly what you said!"

"No, you idiot," he replied. "You got it mixed up. I said tie up the guard and blow the safe!"

FARMER AND THE LAWYER

A big city lawyer went duck hunting in rural Queensland. He shot a bird, but it fell into a farmer's field on the other side of a fence.

As the lawyer climbed over the fence, an elderly farmer drove up on his tractor and asked him what he was doing.

The lawyer responded, "I shot a duck and it fell in this field, and I'm going to retrieve it."

The old farmer replied, "This is my property, and you're not coming over here."

The indignant lawyer said, "Look I'm one of the best trial lawyers in Australia and, if you don't let me get that duck, I'll sue you and take everything you own."

The old farmer smiled and said, "Apparently, you don't know how disputes are resolved in the outback. We settle small disagreements like this with the 'Three Kick Rule.'"

The lawyer asked, "What's the 'Three Kick Rule'?"

The farmer replied, "Well, because the dispute occurs on

my land, I go first. I kick you three times and then you kick me three times and so on, back and forth until someone gives up."

The lawyer quickly thought about the proposed contest and decided that he could easily take on the old codger. He agreed to abide by the local custom.

The old farmer slowly climbed down from the tractor and walked up to the barrister. His first kick planted the tip of his heavy steel toed work boot into the lawyer's groin and dropped him to his knees!

His second kick to the midriff sent the lawyer's last meal gushing from his mouth. The lawyer was on all fours when the farmer's third kick to his rear end, sent him face-first into a fresh cowpat.

Summoning every bit of his will and remaining strength the lawyer very slowly managed to get to his feet. Wiping his face with the arm of his jacket, he said, "Okay, you old fart. Now it's my turn."

The old farmer smiled and said, "Nah, I give up. You can have the duck."

FURNITURE SHOPPING

The Prime Minister was seen going to a furniture store. He was surrounded by his bodyguards, and everyone immediately took notice of the unusual occurrence. They looked closer and they saw who it was. Everyone was in awe. "Why would the Prime Minister be going in there?" they all asked each other. "He should have his workers do it for him."

Finally, one man asked the PM, "What are you doing in this little store of ours?" To which the PM replied, "Oh, everyone has been saying that I should get a new cabinet."

HOLY MAX

Each Friday night after work, Max would fire up the barbie in his backyard and cook some steak. All of Max's neighbours were Catholic and as it was Lent, they were forbidden from eating meat on a Friday. The delicious aroma from the grilled steaks wafted over the neighbourhood and was causing such a problem for the Catholic faithful that they finally talked to their priest. The priest visited Max and suggested that he become a Catholic. After several classes and much study, Max attended Mass and as the priest sprinkled holy water over him, he said,

"You were born a Lutheran and raised a Lutheran but now you are a Catholic." Max's neighbours were relieved, until Friday night arrived and the wonderful aroma of grilled beef filled the neighbourhood again. They called the priest immediately and he rushed to Max's preparing to scold him. On arrival he stopped and watched in amazement. Max was clutching a small bottle of holy water, which he carefully sprinkled over the grilling meat while saying: "You wuz born a cow, you wuz raised a cow but now you is a flathead."

IF YOU DRINK AND DRIVE...

A policeman pulled over a driver for swerving in and out of lanes on the freeway. He told the man to blow breath into a breathalyzer but the man replied, "I can't do that, officer."

"Why not?"

"Because I'm asthmatic. I could have an asthma attack if I blow into that tube."

"Okay, we'll just get a urine sample down at the station." "Can't do that either, officer."

"Why not?"

"Because I'm a diabetic. I could get low blood sugar if I pee in a cup."

"Alright, we can get a blood sample."

"Can't do that either, officer."

"Why not?" "Because I'm a hemophiliac. If I give blood I could die."

"Fine then, just walk this white line."

"Can't do that either, officer."

"Why not?"

"Because I'm drunk."

STRANDED

Two lawyers had been stranded on a deserted island for several months. The only other thing on the island was the tall coconut tree, that provided them their food.

Each day, one of the lawyers climbed to the top of the tree, to see if he could see a rescue boat coming.

One day, the lawyer yelled down from the tree, "Wow! I can't believe my eyes! I don't believe this is true!"

The lawyer on the ground was skeptical and said, "I think you're hallucinating and you should come down right now."

So, the lawyer reluctantly climbed down the tree and told his friend that he had just seen a naked woman floating face up headed toward their island.

The other lawyer started to laugh, thinking his friend had surely lost his mind. But, within a few minutes, up to the beach floated a beautiful naked woman, face up, totally unconscious.

The two lawyers went over to her and one said to the other, "You know, we've been on this island for months now without a woman. It's been a long time... do you think we should... you know... screw her?"

The other lawyer glanced down at the totally naked woman and asked, "Out of what?"

THE COW

Farmer Joe was injured in an accident and decided to sue the trucking company responsible. for the accident. In court the company's fancy lawyer was questioning Farmer Joe.

"Didn't you say at the scene of the accident, 'I'm fine,'" asked the lawyer. Farmer Joe responded, "Well, I'll tell you what happened. I had just loaded my favorite mule Bessie into the..."

"I didn't ask for any details," the lawyer interrupted, "just answer the question. Did you not say at the scene of the accident, "I'm fine!'?"

Farmer Joe said, "Well, I had just got Bessie into the trailer and as I was driving down the road…"

The lawyer interrupted again and said, "Judge, I am trying to establish the fact that, at the scene of the accident, this man told the highway patrolman on the scene that he was fine. Now several weeks after the accident he is trying to sue my client. I believe he is a fraud. Please tell him to simply answer the question."

By this time the judge was fairly interested in Farmer Joe's answer and said to the lawyer, "I'd like to hear what he has to say."

Joe thanked the Judge and proceeded. "Well, as I was saying, I had just loaded Bessie into the trailer and was driving her down the highway when this huge semi-truck and trailer ran the stop sign and smacked my truck right in the side.

CAR SMASH

A lawyer's car stalled on the side of the freeway. As he was getting out to see what was the matter, a reckless driver swerved, taking off the whole car door and knocking the lawyer to the ground. A passing police car pulled over.

As the policeman got out he heard the lawyer shouting, "My Mercedes, my brand new Mercedes!" As the policeman approached he was shocked to notice the lawyer's right arm missing.

"Do you realise your arm is gone?" asked the policeman.

The lawyer, stunned, began to scream, "My Rolex, my brand new Rolex!"

REDEMPTION

Two young guys were picked up by the cops for smoking dope and appeared in court on Friday before the judge. The judge said, "You seem like nice young men, and I'd like to give you a second chance rather than jail time. I want you to go out this weekend and try to show others the evils of drug use and get them to give up drugs forever. I'll see you back in court Monday."

Monday, the two guys were back in court, and the judge said to the first one, "How did you do over the weekend?"

"Well, your Honor, I persuaded 24 people to give up drugs forever."

"24 people? That's wonderful. What did you tell them?"

"I used a diagram, your Honor. I drew two circles like this," he proceeded to draw two circles: O o

"I told them this (the big circle) is your brain before drugs and this (small circle) is your brain after drugs."

"That's admirable," said the judge. "And you, how did you do?" he asked the second boy.

"Well, your Honor, I persuaded 236 people to give up drugs forever."

"236 people! That's amazing! How did you manage to do that?"

"Well, I used a similar approach." He drew the same circles,

"I said (pointing to the small circle) this is your arsehole before prison..."

BRIBERY

A bloke due to appear in court was discussing his case in the bar. His drinking mate advised, "If you want to get off, send the judge a case of whiskey."

The defendant discussed this with his legal advisor the next morning. "On no account do anything like that," said his solicitor. "We've got a thin argument already without complicating it with a bribe."

To the solicitor's astonishment the bloke won his case. "We would have lost if you had sent that case of whiskey."

"Oh, but I did," said the bloke. "I just put the other bloke's name on the card."

SON OF A...

A man wrongly accused of stealing was tried for the final time and was found guilty. Just before he was taken away, the man looked the judge in the eye and said, "Would it be okay if I called you a son of a b★★★★?"

The judge's face went red and he roared, "It most certainly would not! I'd add another two years onto your sentence!"

The defendant nodded and then asked, "Would it be okay if I thought you were a son of a b★★★★?"

The judge was becoming very annoyed but replied, "Yes, I

suppose that would be okay. I obviously have no control over your thoughts." The defendant smiled and said, "Well, in that case, judge, I think you are a son of a b★★★★"

ACCIDENTS...

An old man lay sprawled across three seats in the picture theatre. When the usher came by and noticed this, he whispered to the old man, "Sorry sir, but you're only allowed one seat."

The old man just groaned but didn't budge. The usher became impatient, "Sir, if you don't get up I'll have to call the manager." Once again, the old man just groaned.

The usher marched briskly back up the aisle, and shortly returned with the manager. Together the two of them repeatedly tried to move the old dishevelled man, but with no success. Finally, they summoned the police.

The officer surveyed the situation briefly then asked, "All right mate what's your name?"

"Fred," the old man moaned.

"Where ya from, Fred?" asked the police officer.

With terrible pain in his voice, and without moving a muscle, Fred replied, "The balcony."

NANCY KNOWS

A police officer pulls over a speeding car. The officer says, "You're 20km over the 100km speed limit."

The male driver replies. "Officer I had it on cruise control at 100, perhaps your radar gun needs checking."

The driver's wife says, "Darling you know that this car doesn't have cruise control."

"Shut up Nancy," snaps the driver as the officer writes a ticket. As he hands the ticket to the driver, he says, "You're not wearing your seat belt. That's a $50 fine," and writes another ticket.

"But officer I took it off when you stopped me, so that I could get my licence from my back pocket."

Nancy says, "Darling, you never wear your seat belt when driving."

The driver is furious and shouts, "Nancy shut up!" as the police officer writes the third ticket.

The officer asks the woman, "Madam does your husband always speak to you like that?"

"Only when he's been drinking."

HOLY MOLY

After packing the Pope's luggage into the limo, the driver notices the Pope is still standing on the curb.

"Excuse me, Your Holiness," says the driver, "Would you please take your seat so we can leave?"

"Well, I was wondering if you could do me a favour," says the Pope, "they never let me drive at the Vatican when I was a cardinal, and I'd very much like to drive today."

"I'm sorry, Your Holiness, but I cannot let you do that. I'd lose my job! What if something should happen?" protests the driver, wishing he'd never gone to work that morning.

"Who's going to tell?" says the Pope with a smile.

Reluctantly, the driver climbs in the back as the Pope clambers in behind the wheel. The driver quickly regrets his decision when, after exiting the airport, the Pontiff floors it, accelerating the limo to 150 kph.

"Please slow down, Your Holiness!" begs the worried driver, but the Pope keeps the pedal down until they hear sirens.

"Oh, dear God, I'm going to lose my licence – and my job!" moans the driver.

The Pope pulls over and rolls down the window as the policeman approaches, but the policeman takes one look at him, goes back to his motorcycle, and radios headquarters.

"I need to talk to the Police Chief," says the policeman.

The Chief gets on the radio and the policeman tells him that he's stopped a limo going 155 kph.

"So book him," says the Chief.

"I don't think we want to do that, he's really important," says the policeman.

The Chief exclaims, "All the more reason!"

"No, I mean really important," insists the policeman.

The Chief then asks, "Who do you have – the mayor?"

The policeman says, "Bigger."

The chief then asks, "The President?"

The policeman says, "Bigger."

"Well," says the Chief, "who is it?"

The policeman says, "I think it's God!"

The Chief is even more puzzled and curious, "What makes you think it's God?"

The policeman says, "His chauffeur is the Pope!"

ON TRIAL

A man was on trial for murder. There was strong evidence suggesting he was guilty, but no corpse had been found.

The defence lawyer knowing that his client would probably be found guilty decided to use a trick.

"Ladies and gentlemen of the jury, I have a surprise for you all," the lawyer said. "In one minute, the person presumed dead in this case will walk into this courtroom." He looked toward the courtroom door. As did all the amazed jurors.

The lawyer checked his watch. A minute had passed. But no one had entered the court room.

At last, the lawyer said, "Members of the jury I invented the previous statement. No corpse has been found. But you all looked at the door eagerly waiting to see the person presumed dead enter. It is clear that you have a reasonable doubt as to whether anyone was killed, and therefore, you must in all honesty return a verdict of not guilty."

The jury retired to decide on their verdict. Soon after they returned and pronounced the accused guilty.

"How can you justify this?" asked the lawyer. "It was clear that you had some doubt or you would not have stared at the door."

The jury foreman responded, "That's true, we looked but the accused didn't!"

U TURN

Manfred was driving home one evening when a traffic camera flashed. He thought it strange because he wasn't exceeding the speed limit. So to check he was right, he did a u-turn and went through the same place making sure that he was driving within the limit. But the camera flashed again. This was weird he thought, so he did another u-turn and went even slower through the same spot again, and sure enough, the camera flashed yet again. What a joke! He repeated the exercise a fourth time, this time laughing out loud as the camera flashed. He and his wife had a chuckle about it that evening.

A few weeks later, he got four traffic fines - for driving without his head lights.

HELPFUL TIPS

All those doomsdayers about Climate Change are bad sports. They're not talking about the opportunities Climate Change will bring. As the planet heats up there's going to be some cool new jobs. For instance: Swimming Instructors, Gondola Operators, Stilts Manufacturers, Bleached Coral Painters, Political Bodyguards, Political Hitmen, Insurance Assessors, Border Security Guards, and Raindance Choreographers.

Tips from *Green and Proud Of It* by Eartha Waters.
A. In winter wear an extra layer of clothing. Put your heater down to 21 degrees, so that you don't use too much energy to

warm yourself, particularly with that nasty coal.

I thought being green and proud of it, I'd put my heater down to 10 degrees and put on ten layers of clothing instead. I don't mind looking cuddly.

B. Check your ecological footprint. Go onto the Internet and work out your ecological footprint. How much impact you're making on the planet, with what you buy, trips you make, water and energy you use and that sort of thing.

I was shocked. If everyone lived like I used to live, we would need about seven planets. I thought – I know what I'll do. I'm going to make my footprint smaller. So I bunch up my toes and wear smaller shoes now. It does pinch a bit and I can't walk too far but it's worth it.

C. Eat less red meat. So I thought that's it. No more red meat for me. I went to the butcher to see if there were any other kinds of meat I could eat. And there were. They were all pink!

D. If it blinks, switch it off! Now that is hard because I have a dear friend Violet, who blinks all the time. When she visits, how can I tell her to switch it off?

E. Short efficient showers. My shower is quite tall. I mean it reaches up to the ceiling. So it can't be efficient. I have asked my hubby to put in a false ceiling, so that the shower can become short and efficient. So he's added that to his long list of things to do.

F. Buy less. When you buy less you use less energy or water or forests and so on. And you also save money.

So I use my friends' things. But it's very strange. My friends don't seem to like it. They grumble about this. They're not very green are they?

G. Look for the stars. Well I went outside every night and looked for the stars. My hubby got angry because I was spending all my evenings outside. Then he explained to me that 'look for the stars' means when you buy whitegoods you have to get those with the most stars, because they use less energy and water.

H. Be political to make big changes. So I'm going to see our Prime Minister right now and show him how to be green and proud of it.

DOG ACT

A dog ran into a butcher's shop and grabbed a roast off the counter. Fortunately, the butcher recognised the dog as belonging to a neighbour of his, who happened to be a lawyer.

Incensed at the theft, the butcher called him up and said, "Hey, if your dog stole a roast from my butcher shop, would you be liable for the cost of the meat?"

The lawyer replied, "Of course, how much was the roast?"

"$7.98." A few days later the butcher received a cheque in the mail for $7.98. Attached to it was an invoice that read: Legal Consultation Service: $150.

HAMMERED

The judge says to a double-homicide defendant, "You're charged with beating your wife to death with a hammer."

A voice at the back of the courtroom yells out, "You b★★★★!" The judge says, "You're also charged with beating your mother-in-law to death with a hammer."

The voice in the back of the courtroom yells out, "You rotten b★★★★!" The judge stops and says to the in the back of the courtroom. "Sir, I can understand your anger and frustration at these crimes, but no more outbursts from you, or I'll charge you with contempt. Is that understood?"

They stand up and say, "I'm sorry, Your Honour, but for fifteen years I've lived next door to that creep, and every time I asked to borrow a hammer, he said he didn't have one."

THE CATCH

A lawyer is on a long flight and is bored. So he decides to have a game at the expense of the man sitting beside him.

The lawyer asks him if he would like to play a game. The man is tired and just wants to take a nap, so he politely declines, and tries to catch a few winks. The lawyer persists, and says that the game is a lot of fun.

"I ask you a question, and if you don't know the answer, you pay me only $5. You ask me one, and if I don't know the answer, I pay you $500," he says.

This catches the man's attention and to keep the lawyer quiet, he agrees to play the game. The lawyer asks the first question, "What's the distance from the Earth to the Moon?" The man doesn't say a word, reaches in his pocket, pulls out a five-dollar bill, and hands it to the lawyer.

Now, it's the man's turn. He asks the lawyer, "What goes up a hill with three legs, and comes down with four?" The lawyer uses his laptop and searches all references he can find on the net. He sends emails to smart people he knows, but to no avail. After an hour of searching while his companion is sleeping, he gives up. He wakes up his neighbour and hands him $500. The man pockets the $500 and goes back to sleep.

The lawyer is desperate to know the answer. He wakes up the man and asks, "Well, what goes up a hill with three legs and comes down with four?"

The man reaches in his pocket, hands the lawyer $5 and goes back to sleep.

AUSSIE, AUSSIE, AUSSIE

OI, OI, OI!

GRUMPY COACH

A famous football coach who was well known for his terrible eyesight and short-sightedness coupled with a very bad temper was conducting a training session and noticed that the players were somewhat listless and inattentive.

Losing his temper he shouted,

"You at the back of the room! What should the full-back do if he's playing on the right and there's a break through on the opposite side of the field?"

"I don't know," said the chap at the back.

"Well then, can you tell me the rules governing the defence position when a penalty is being taken?"

"I don't know," was the reply.

"I taught you that only yesterday!" bellowed the coach, "Didn't you hear what I said?"

"I wasn't here," said the man.

"Where were you then?"

"I was having a few drinks with some friends."

The coach turned purple. "You have the audacity to tell me that! How do you expect to improve?"

"I don't, coach. I'm an electrician and I just came in here to fix the lights."

SCORING PROBLEMS

Three golfers were going at it hammer and tongs while a fourth lay dead in a bunker. A club official was called.

"What's the problem here?" he demanded.

"Well," said one player, "my partner's had a stroke, and these two bastards want to add it to my score."

SAME OLD

The Grand Final was being shown on television and Jack was yelling and shouting as loudly as the fans at the ground.

"I can't understand what all the fuss is about," said his wife as she handed him a cup of tea. "I thought they already decided who the champions were last year."

LOSE THE LOSERS

A desperate coach, whose team had lost twelve consecutive games, rang a colleague for advice on training methods.

"I'll tell you what you should do," said his mate. "Take the team out on a 10km run every day."

"What's the point of that?" asked the coach.

"Today's Monday," was the reply. "By Saturday, they'll be 60kms away and you can forget all about them."

MERV AND THE MCG

Merv has two tickets to the best seats at the MCG for the footy finals. After he sits down, Gary comes along and asks if anyone is sitting in the seat next to him.

"No," Merv says, "that seat isn't taken."

"This is incredible!" says Gary, "who in their right mind would have a seat like this, at the footy finals and not use it?"

Merv says, "Well, actually, the seat belongs to me. My wife was supposed to come with me, but she passed away. This is the first final we haven't been together since we got married."

"Oh... I'm sorry to hear that. That's terrible. I guess you couldn't find someone else? A friend or relative or even a neighbour to take the seat?"

Merv shakes his head. "No, they're all at the funeral."

GONE GOLFIN'

Bert was a keen golfer and was always the first to arrive at the course and never let illness or bad weather stop him. One day while playing a round with his friend and just as he was just about to score a birdie, a funeral procession went past and he stopped and bent his head. Fred couldn't believe it it, his friend never paused before such an amazing shot. He asked Bert why he had paused and bowed his head,

"She was a good wife," explained Bert.

FOOTBALL HEAVEN

Two old mates were reflecting on life and started talking about footy. Finally they were discussing whether or not footy was played in heaven. After a while they came to an agreement. Whoever died first would come back and tell the other if they played footy in heaven. Eventually one of the men died. About two weeks later as the other man was in bed for the night, his friend came to see him.

The man asked, "Hey old mate is there footy in heaven?"

His mate answered, "I've got good news and bad news. The good news is that there is footy in heaven. The bad news is you've been selected for tomorrow's team."

CALM BEFORE THE STORM

Every Saturday morning Colin has got up early, quietly dressed so as not to wake his wife, picked up his golf bag and slipped quietly into the garage. This Saturday after loading his car he backed out into the torrential downpour. The gale was blowing so hard that he drove back into the garage and checked the weather on his iPhone. The forecast was the same all day. So he texted his mates and said he wouldn't be playing that day. He tiptoed back into the bedroom, undressed, and slipped back into bed. Colin nuzzled into his wife's inviting back, whispering, "The weather's dreadful."

His wife of 10 years replied, "Imagine, my idiot of a husband is playing golf in that."

HUNTING

A couple of hunters were out in the woods when one of them fell to the ground. His friend bent down to check him and found that he wasn't breathing. He pulled out his mobile phone and dialled the emergency services. He gasped to the operator, "My friend is dead! What can I do?"

The operator, in a calm soothing voice, replied, "Just take it easy. I can help. First, let's make sure he's dead."

The phone went silent.

"Hello, are you still there?" the operator called down the line. Just then she heard a loud bang.

The hunter's voice came back though the line, "OK, he's dead. Now what?"

CUT BACKS

Grant was having a real bad day on the golf course. After he missed a twelve-inch putt, his mate Joe asked him what the problem was.

"It's my wife," said Grant dejectedly. "As you know she's taken up golf. And since she's been playing, she's cut my sex down to once a week."

"Well, you should think yourself lucky," said Joe. "She's cut some of us out all together."

FRIENDS OF THE UMPIRE

The football club dance was in full swing when a group of strangers arrived and demanded admission to the dance.
"May I see your tickets, please?" said the club secretary.

"We haven't got any tickets," said one of the men.

"We're friends of the umpire." announced another.

"Get out of here!" said the club secretary. "Whoever heard of an umpire with friends!"

LION TAMER

A circus owner puts an ad out for a lion tamer. One applicant is Bret a retired footballer in his sixties and the other is Melinda, a gorgeous blonde in her twenties.

The circus owner tells them, "I'm not going to sugar coat it. This is a ferocious lion. He ate my last tamer, so you two had better be good or you're history. Here's your equipment – chair, whip and a gun. Who wants to try out first?"

Melinda says, "I'll go first." She walks past the chair, the whip, and the gun, and steps right into the lion's cage. The lion starts to snarl and pant and begins to charge her. About halfway there, she throws open her coat revealing her beautiful body. The lion stops dead in his tracks, sheepishly crawls up to her and starts licking her feet and ankles. He continues to lick and kiss her entire body for several minutes and then rests his head at her feet. The circus owner's jaw is on the floor.

He says, "I've never seen a display like that in my life."

He then turns to Bret and asks, "Can you top that?"

The tough old footballer replies, "No problem, just get that lion out of there."

OH, ED

Two couples were playing golf. Ed's ball stopped right in front of a shed beside the course. His pal Mark came up with a brilliant idea to open the doors either end of the shed so that Ed could drive the ball through the shed. He took an almighty swing and the ball flew through. Unfortunately it hit his wife Amy and killed her. It was about a year before Ed began to recover from the shock.

Mark said, "Ed you've got to try to live again. Play golf with me." Ed was very nervous but eventually gave in. However, his ball again stopped just before that shed. Bert said, "Don't worry Ed I'll open both doors."

"Don't!" screamed Ed. "That cost me a stroke last time!"

DRESS SENSE

Do you know that when a woman wears a leather dress, a man's heart beats quicker, his throat gets dry, he goes weak in the knees and he begins to think irrationally.

Ever wonder why?

It's because she smells like a new golf bag.

THE EX WIFE

Tom decided to tie the knot with his long-time girlfriend Jane. One evening, after the honeymoon, he was cleaning his golf clubs in the garage. Jane was standing beside him watching. After a long silence she finally spoke,

"Honey, I've been thinking, now that we're married, I think it's time you quit golfing and hanging out at the club, and drinking with your friends."

Tom looked horrified.

Jane said "Darling, what's wrong?"

Tom replied "For a minute you sounded like my ex-wife."

"Ex-wife!" Jane screamed "I didn't know you were married before!"

"I wasn't."

HAPPY ANNIVERSARY

Bob and Cath met at a party and Bob fell headlong in love with Cath and asked her out.

He took her to clubs, restaurants, concerts and movies and after a month he was convinced that she was the one for him.

On the anniversary of their first meeting, Bob took Cath to a beachfront restaurant.

He said, "I'm very much in love with you. But there's something you must know before I ask you an important question. I must tell you that I'm obsessed with golf. I play golf, I read about golf, I watch golf on TV. I eat, sleep, and breathe golf. If that's going to be a problem for us, you'd better say so now!"

Cath looked into Bob's eyes, took a deep breath and said, "Bob I love you and I can live with that, because I love golf too.

But, also I have to be totally honest with you. I'm a hooker."

Bob said, "That's probably because you're not keeping your wrists straight when you hit the ball."

CRIKEY, DOCTOR!

LACK OF SEX DRIVE

Peter, who was in his seventies was concerned about his lack of sex drive and consulted his doctor. "Well, what would you expect at your age?" the doctor replied. But old Peter was still worried. "Jack, my next door neighbour, is over 80, he says he gets it every night." The doc thought for a moment. "Well, why don't you say it too?"

WORK AS YOUR SALVATION

When Joe's wife left him he got so depressed that his doctor sent him to see a psychiatrist. Joe told the psychiatrist his troubles and said, "Life isn't worth living."
"Don't be stupid, Joe," said the psychiatrist. "Let work be your salvation. I want you to totally submerge yourself in your work. Now, what do you do for a living?"
    "I clean septic tanks," Joe replied.

BAD AND VERY BAD NEWS

The doctor said to the patient, "I've got bad news and very bad news."
    "Give me the bad news first," the patient said.
    "You've only got 24 hours to live."
    "What's the very bad news then?" asked the patient.
    "I should have told you yesterday."

UNETHICAL

The beautiful patient who was extremely satisfied with her psychiatrist said, "Kiss me! Please kiss me!"

"No," said the psychiatrist, "that's unethical, Miss. I shouldn't even be having sex with you."

FREE ASSOCIATION

A psychiatrist interviewing a patient said, "I want to try some free association. Just answer the following questions as quickly as you can — say the first thing that comes into your head. Now, what is it that a man does standing up, a lady sitting down, and a dog on three legs?"

"Shakes hands," said the patient at once.

"Good," said the psychiatrist. "Now, what does a dog do in the garden that you wouldn't want to step in?"

"Digs a hole," said the patient without hesitation.

"Right," said the psychiatrist. "And, finally, what is it that sticks stiffly out of your pyjamas when you wake up in the morning?"

"Your head," said the patient.

"Excellent," said the psychiatrist. "Your responses are perfectly normal. You'd be surprised at some of the weird answers I get!"

ASTHMA

The doctor looked in on the little old lady he had been treating for asthma. He checked her over, asked a few questions and listened to her croaky replies.

"What about the wheeze?" he asked.

"Oh, fine," she replied. "I went three times last night!"

GOOD OR BAD NEWS

"Mrs Anderson, I have some very good news for you." The doctor had finished his examination and with a smile on his face. "Miss Anderson," she corrected.

The doctor continued, "Miss Anderson, I have some very bad news for you!"

SEXUAL DISORDER

An very embarrassed man went to the doctor.

"Doctor," the man said, "I have a sexual problem. I can't get it up for my wife anymore."

"Bring her back with you tomorrow and let me see what I can do." The next day, the worried fellow returned with his wife. "Take off your clothes, Mrs Jones," the GP said. "Now turn all the way around. Lie down please. Uh-huh, I see. Okay, you may put your clothes back on."

The doctor took Mr Jones aside. "You're in perfect health," he said. "Your wife didn't give me an erection either."

GRUDGE PREGNANCY

A sailor was confused when his wife became pregnant so he went to the doctor.

"She can't be pregnant," he said. "I haven't seen her for two years."

"It's what we call a grudge pregnancy," explained the doctor.

"What's that?" the sailor asked.

"It's when someone has it in for you."

WITCH DOCTOR

Angus sent a letter to his old mother:

Dear Mother,

I am sending you some pills that a witch doctor gave me, if you take one it will take years off you.

A few weeks later Angus came home and there was a beautiful young woman outside his house rocking a pram in which lay a baby.

"Where's my mother?" he asked.

"Don't be silly Angus," she said. "I'm your mother, those pills you sent were marvellous."

"Imagine," said Angus, "one pill and you're as beautiful as anyone could be and what's more you were able to have a baby. Lord but they must be powerful."

"You idiot," she cried, "that's not my baby. That's your father, he took two."

THE DELIGHTFUL DENTIST

I was sitting in the waiting room for my first appointment with a new dentist. On the wall was his dental diploma, with his full name. It brought back memories of a tall handsome dark-haired boy with the same name in my secondary school class about 35 years ago.

Could he be the same person that I had a secret crush on all those years ago? On seeing him, I quickly dropped that thought. This balding, grey haired man with the deeply lined face was far too old to have been my classmate. But after he examined my teeth I asked him anyway if he'd attended Burwood High School.

"Yes I did," he smiled.

"When did you leave?" I asked.

It was the same year that I'd left!

"You were in my class!" I exclaimed.

He looked at me closely. Then that ugly, old, balding, wrinkled, decrepit, drongo asked, "What did you teach?"

ANAL INTERCOURSE

An anxious woman went to see to her doctor.

"Doctor," she asked nervously, "can you get pregnant from anal intercourse?"

"Certainly," replied the doctor, "Where do you think lawyers come from!"

DEPRESSION

Tracy, the pert and pretty nurse, took her troubles to a resident psychiatrist in the hospital where she worked.

"Doctor, you must help me," she pleaded. "It has gotten so that every time I date one of the young doctors here, I end up in bed with him. And then afterward, I feel guilty and depressed for a week."

"I see," nodded the psychiatrist. "And you, no doubt, want me to strengthen your willpower and resolve in this matter."

"For God's sake, no!" exclaimed the nurse. "I want you to fix it so I won't feel guilty and depressed afterward."

THE MYSTERY RED-HEAD

Megan and Simon both had black hair, but when their first child was born, he was a redhead. Being suspicious, Simon consulted his doctor.

"There has never been a redhead in either my family or my wife's, so why should my son have red hair?" he asked.

"How long have you been married?" asked the doctor.

"Ten years."

"How often do you and your wife have sex?"

"Two or three times a year," replied Simon.

"That explains it," said the doctor. "You're rusty."

A NEW MAN

A man woke up in the hospital bandaged from head to foot. The doctor came in and said, "Ah, I see you've regained consciousness. Now you probably won't remember, but you were in a huge pile-up on the freeway. You're going to be okay, you'll walk again and everything, but your penis was severed in the accident and we couldn't find it."

The man groaned, but the doctor continued, "You've got $9000 in insurance compensation coming and we now have the technology to build a new penis. They work great but they don't come cheap. It's $1000 an inch."

The man perked up.

"So," the doctor told him, "you must decide how many inches you want. But this is something you should discuss with your wife. If you had a five incher before and get a nine incher now she might be a bit put out. If you had a nine incher before and you decide to only invest in a five incher now, she might be disappointed. It's important that she plays a role in helping you make a decision."

The man agreed to talk it over with his wife. The doctor returned the next day, "So, have you spoken with your wife?"

"Yes, I have," says the patient.

"And has she helped you make a decision?"

"Yes," the man informed him. "We're getting granite counter tops."

PENIS ENVY

A man went to the doctor about his lisp. While examining him, the doctor saw that he had an enormous penis and told him that it was the reason for his lisp.

"If you transplant this one for an ordinary one, no doubt the lisp will disappear," the doctor said.

The man had the operation. His lisp disappeared, but also his luck with the women. He got so fed up with this that he went back to the doctor and asked if the operation could be reversed.

"Thorry," said the doctor, "but that'th impothible."

HEART CONDITION

The doctor had examined old Jack's heart and told him he must give up smoking, drinking and sex.

After much protesting by Jack, the doctor relented.

"Okay, one cigarette only after meals, and no more than two glasses of light beer a day."

"What about sex?" pressed Jack.

"Very occasionally," said the doctor, "and only with your wife because it's important to avoid any excitement."

NICE RIDE

A 60 year old man on a motor scooter pulls up next to a doctor in his sleek car at a street light. The scooter driver looks at the shiny car and asks, "What kind of car ya got there, sonny?"

The doctor replies, "A Bugatti Veyron, and it cost two and half million dollars."

"That's a lot of money," says the scooter driver. "Why's it so pricey?"

"Because it can do up to 267 miles an hour!" says the proud doctor. The scooter driver asks, "Mind if I peek inside?"

"No problem," replies the doctor.

So the scooter driver pokes his head in the window and looks around. Then, sitting back on his scooter, he says, "That's a pretty nice car, all right, but I'll stick with my scooter!"

Just then the light changes and the doctor decides to show the old man just what his car can do. He floors it, and within 30 seconds the speedometer reads 120 mph.

Suddenly, he notices a dot in his rear view mirror. It seems to be getting closer! He slows down to see what it could be and whooooooosh! Something whips by him going much faster!

"What could be going faster than my Bugatti?" the doctor asks himself. He presses harder on the accelerator and takes the Bugatti up to 150 mph. Then ahead of him, he sees that it's the old man on the scooter!

Amazed that the scooter could pass his Bugatti, the doctor gives it more petrol and passes the scooter at 200 mph. He's feeling pretty good until he looks in his mirror and sees the old man gaining on him again! Astounded, the doctor floors the accelerator and takes the Bugatti all the way to 260 mph.

Not ten seconds later, he sees the scooter bearing down on him again! The Bugatti is flat out, and there's nothing he can do! Suddenly, the scooter ploughs into the back of his Bugatti.

Demolishing the rear end. The doctor stops and jumps out and amazingly the old man is still alive. He runs to the smashed up man and says, "I'm a doctor... is there anything I can do for you?"

The old man whispers, "Unhook my braces from your side view mirror."

PHENOMENON

Fear swept a city hospital's intensive care unit as patients always died in the same bed every Monday at 10 a.m. regardless of their medical problem. This concerned the doctors, some thinking it might have a supernatural cause. Word spread about this phenomenon. Experts from around the world gathered on a Monday to try and find the cause. Shortly before 10 a.m. they assembled some holding crosses and Bibles to protect them from Satan. At the stroke of 10 a.m. in came the part-time cleaner, Doug Thompson. He made straight for the bed, unplugged the life support system, and plugged in the vacuum cleaner...

HEAVEN??

An elderly man lay dying in his hospital bed. While suffering the agonies of impending death, he suddenly smelled the aroma of his favourite fruit scones wafting up the stairs.

He gathered his remaining strength, and lifted himself from

the bed. Leaning on the wall, he slowly made his way out of the bedroom, and with even greater effort, gripping the railing with both hands, he crawled downstairs.

With laboured breath, he leaned against the door-frame, gazing into the kitchen. Were it not for death's agony, he would have thought himself already in heaven, for there, spread out upon the kitchen table were literally hundreds of his favourite fruit scones.

Was it heaven? Or was it one final act of love from his devoted wife of sixty years, seeing to it that he left this world a happy man?

Mustering one great final effort, he threw himself towards the table, landing on his knees in rumpled posture. His aged and withered hand trembled towards a scone at the edge of the table, when it was suddenly smacked by his wife with a wooden spoon.

"Get off!" she shouted. "They're for the funeral."

WHATEVER SUITS BEST

A man who had just died is delivered to the mortuary wearing an expensive, expertly tailored grey suit. The mortician asks the widow how she would like the body dressed. He points out that the man looks good in the grey suit he's wearing.

The widow however, says that she always thought her husband looked his best in blue and that she wants him in a blue suit. She gives the mortician a blank cheque and says, "I don't care what it costs, but please have my husband in a blue suit for the viewing."

The widow returns the next day for the wake.

To her delight, she finds her husband dressed in a gorgeous blue suit with a subtle chalk stripe; the suit fits him perfectly.

She says to the mortician, "Whatever this cost, I'm very satisfied. You did an excellent job and I'm very grateful. How much did you spend?"

To her astonishment, the mortician returns the blank cheque.

"There's no charge," he says.

"No really, I must compensate you for the cost of that exquisite blue suit," she says.

"Honestly madam," the mortician says, "it cost nothing. You see, a deceased man of about your husband's size was brought in shortly after you left yesterday and he was wearing an attractive blue suit. I asked his wife if she minded him going to his grave wearing a grey suit instead and she said it made no difference as long as he looked nice. So I just switched the heads."

EXERCISE FOR PEOPLE OVER 40.

Start by standing on a comfortable surface, where you have plenty of room on each side. With a 1 kilo potato bag in each hand, extend your arms straight out from your sides and hold them there as long as you can. Try to reach a full minute, and then relax. Each day you'll find that you can hold this position for just a bit longer. After a couple of weeks, move up to 5 kilo potato bags. Then try 25 kilo potato bags and then eventually, try to lift a 50 kilo potato bag in each hand and hold your arms straight for more than a full minute.

...After you feel confident at that level, put a potato in each bag.

Some more tips:

A. Walking can add minutes to your life, this enables you at 85 years old to spend an additional 5 months in a nursing home at $4,000 a month.
B. My grandfather started walking three km a day at 65. Now he's 80 and we don't know where the hell he is.
C. My friend told me the only reason she took up exercise was to hear heavy breathing again.
D. I joined a gym a year ago for $500 and haven't lost an ounce. Apparently you have to attend the gym.
E. I like long walks, especially when they're taken by people who annoy me.
F. I have flabby thighs, but fortunately my stomach covers them.

EXERCISES

Many women are afraid of their first mammogram, but there's no need. By spending a few minutes doing the following exercises at home daily for a week before the exam, you'll be totally prepared.

Exercise one:

Open your refrigerator door and insert one breast in the fridge. Slam shut the door as hard as possible and lean on it. Hold that position for five seconds. Repeat again in case the first time wasn't effective enough.

Exercise two:

Go to your garage at 3 a.m. when the temperature of the cement floor is just perfect. Take off all your clothes and lie comfortably on the floor with one breast wedged under the rear tyre of the car.

Ask a friend to slowly back the car up until your breast is sufficiently flattened and chilled. Turn over and repeat with the other breast.

Exercise three:

Freeze two metal bookends overnight. Strip to the waist. Invite a stranger into the room. Ask the stranger to position the bookends on either side of one of your breasts, then to smash the bookends together as hard as she can. Repeat with the other breast. Make an appointment with the stranger to do it again next year.

HEARING PROBLEMS

An elderly man called Reginald had serious hearing problems for several years. He went to a doctor who fitted him for a set of hearing aids that allowed Reginald to hear 100 percent. After a month Reginald went back to the doctor for a check and was told, "Your hearing is perfect. Your family must be really pleased that you can hear again."

Reginald replied, "Oh, I haven't told them yet. I just sit around and listen to the conversations. I've changed my will three times!"

PARDON?

Bert feared his wife Peg wasn't hearing as well as she used to and might need a hearing aid. Not quite sure how to approach her about this, he called the family doctor to discuss the problem. The doctor told him of a simple way to check.

"Stand about 15 metres away from her, and in a normal speaking tone see if she hears you. If not, move to 10 metres, then 5 metres and so on until you get a response."

That evening, Peg was cooking dinner in the kitchen and Bert was in the study about 15 metres away. In a normal tone he asked, "Peg, what's for dinner?"

No response.

So Bert moved closer, about 10 metres from Peg and repeated, "Peg, what's for dinner?" Still no response.

Next, he moved into the dining room where he was about five metres from Peg and asked, "Peg, what's for dinner?" Again, he got no response. He then walked right up behind her. "Peg, what's for dinner?"

"For goodness sake, Bert, for the FOURTH time, CHICKEN!"

CHECK UP

Barry, an 85 year-old man, went to the doctor to have a check up. Several days later, the doctor saw Barry walking down the street with a gorgeous young woman on his arm. On the following Saturday, the doctor bumped into Barry at the local footy ground and said, "You're doing great. I saw you with that gorgeous young woman."

Barry replied, "Just following your orders, Doc: 'Get a hot mamma and be cheerful.'"

"I didn't say that," replied the doctor. "I said, 'You've got a heart murmur; be careful.'"

PRINCE WILLY

Prince William visits an Edinburgh hospital. He enters a ward full of patients with no obvious sign of injury or illness and greets one. The patient replies,

"Fair fa' your honest, sonsie face,
Great chieftain o' the pudding-race!
Aboon them a' yet tak your place,
Painch, tripe, or thairm:
Weel are ye wordy o'a grace
As lang's my airm."

The Prince is confused, so he just smiles and moves on to greet the next patient. The patient responds,

"Some hae meat and canna eat,
And some wad eat that want it;
But we hae meat, and we can eat,
And sae let the Lord be thankit."

Even more confused, the Prince moves on to the next patient, who immediately starts to chant:

"Wee, sleekit, cowrin, tim'rous beastie,
O, what a panic's in thy breastie!
Thou need na start awa sae hasty,

Wi' bickering brattle!
I wad be laith to rin an' chase thee
Wi' murd'ring pattle!"

Now seriously troubled, the Prince turns to the accompanying doctor and asks, "Is this a psychiatric ward?"

"No," replies the doctor, "This is the serious Burns unit."

GOING NUTS

A little old man shuffled slowly into an ice cream parlour in Brisbane, and pulled himself slowly, painfully, up onto a stool. After catching his breath he ordered a banana split. The waitress asked gently, "Crushed nuts?"

"No," he winced, "haemorrhoids."

REGULATIONS

Hospital regulations require a wheelchair for patients being discharged. However, while working as a student nurse, I found one elderly gentleman already dressed and sitting on the bed with a suitcase at his feet, who insisted he didn't need my help to leave the hospital.

After a chat about rules being rules, he reluctantly let me wheel him to the elevator.

On the way down I asked him if his wife was meeting him.

"I don't know," he said. "She's still upstairs in the bathroom changing out of her hospital gown."

PRESCRIPTION PANIC

A distraught senior citizen phoned her doctor's office.

"Is it true that the medication you prescribed has to be taken for the rest of my life?"

"Yes, I'm afraid so," the doctor replied.

There was a moment of silence before the senior lady replied, "I'm wondering, then, just how serious my condition is. Because this prescription is marked 'NO REPEATS'."

TOOTHLESS

The local doctor was making a house call to a little old lady who invited him into the sitting room and asked him to sit while she went to look for her teeth. As he waited he noticed a bowl of peanuts and helped himself to one, then another and as one does, finished the lot before he knew it. Just then the woman came back but unfortunately hadn't been able to find her teeth. The doctor was all apologies about eating all the peanuts and offered to buy her some fresh ones.

"No problems," was her mumbled, toothless reply. "At my age I only suck off the chocolate."

SENIOR SH*TIZENS

It was entertainment night at the Senior Citizens Centre. Bernard the hypnotist explained, "I'm going to hypnotize every member of the audience."

The excitement was almost electric as Bernard withdrew a beautiful antique pocket watch from his coat.

"I want each of you to keep your eyes on this antique watch. It's a very special watch. It's been in my family for 10 generations."

He swung the watch gently back and forth while quietly chanting, "Watch the watch, watch the watch, watch the watch..."

The crowd became mesmerized as the watch swayed back and forth, light gleaming off its polished surface.

A hundred pairs of eyes followed the swaying watch until, suddenly, the chain broke; it slipped from the hypnotist's fingers and fell to the floor, breaking into a hundred pieces.

"SH*T!" said the hypnotist.

It took three days to clean up the Senior Citizens Centre.

MEDICAL OPINION

Some medical friends met annually to shoot rabbits. The GP was the first to spot a rabbit. He took aim then hesitated and decided to ask for a second opinion on whether that was a rabbit or a protected species. The psychiatrist also hesitated as although he thought they were rabbits, perhaps they didn't know they were. But the surgeon didn't hesitate. He grabbed his rifle and with one shot after another killed several animals. He grabbed one to take to his friend, who happened to be a pathologist to confirm that it was indeed a rabbit.

SKILFUL HANDS

A gynaecologist had become fed up with malpractice insurance and was almost burned out. Hoping to try another career where skilful hands would be beneficial, he decided to become a mechanic.

He signed up for evening classes at the local technical college and learned all he could.

When the time for the practical exam approached, the gynaecologist prepared carefully for weeks, and completed the exam with tremendous skill.

When the results came back, he was surprised to find that he had obtained a score of 150 percent. Fearing an error, he called the instructor, saying, "I don't want to appear ungrateful for such an outstanding result, but I was wondering if there had been an error which needed adjusting."

The instructor said, "During the exam, you took the engine apart perfectly, which was worth 50 percent of the total mark. You put the engine back together again perfectly, which is also worth 50 percent of the mark."

The instructor went on to say, "I gave you an extra 50 percent because you did all of it through the muffler."

AUSSIE JOKES

Compiled by Tara Wyllie

ISBN: 9781925367195   Qty

RRP   AU$19.99   .....

Postage within Australia   AU$5.00   .....

TOTAL* $_____

* All prices include GST

Name:...

Address: ....

....

Phone:..

Email: ....

Payment: ❏ Money Order ❏ Cheque ❏ MasterCard ❏ Visa

Cardholder's Name:...

Credit Card Number: ....

Signature:..

Expiry Date: ....

Allow 7 days for delivery.

Payment to: Marzocco Consultancy (ABN 14 067 257 390)
PO Box 12544
A'Beckett Street, Melbourne, 8006
Victoria, Australia
admin@brolgapublishing.com.au

Be Published

Publish through a successful publisher.
Brolga Publishing is represented through:
• **National** book trade distribution, including sales,
marketing & distribution through **Macmillan Australia.**
• **International** book trade distribution to
  • The United Kingdom
  • North America
  • Sales representation in South East Asia
• **Worldwide e-Book distribution**

For details and inquiries, contact:
Brolga Publishing Pty Ltd
PO Box 12544
A'Beckett St VIC 8006

Phone: 0414 608 494
markzocchi@brolgapublishing.com.au
ABN: 46 063 962 443
(Email for a catalogue request)